# HARCOURT SCHOOL PUBLISHERS
# STORYtown

# Turn It Up!

**Harcourt**
SCHOOL PUBLISHERS
www.harcourtschool.com

ISBN 0-15-354538-0
ISBN 978-0-15-354538-2

3 4 5 6 7 8 9 10  179  16 15 14 13 12 11  10 09 08

# CONTENTS

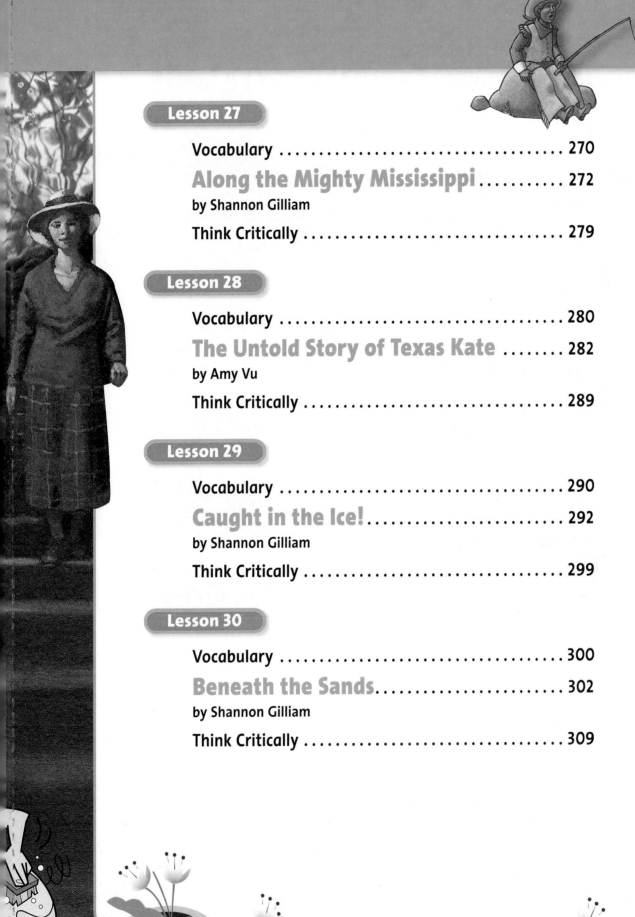

annoyed

depriving

foisted

pact

queasy

venture

# Vocabulary

## Build Robust Vocabulary

Read the story and think about the meanings of the words in dark type.

Dave and Jake plan to have a snack. But Ann comes over. Dave is **annoyed.** He and Jake had made a **pact** not to like Ann.

Dave and Jake grab some cake. They cram the cake down fast. Jake looks **queasy.**

Dave looks over at Ann. "We are **depriving** Ann of cake, Jake." But the cake can't be **foisted** on Ann. She said, "No, thanks! I pass. This is all your **venture**!"

Will Dave and Jake be pals with Ann? Who will have the last of the cake?

© Harcourt

**Write the Vocabulary Word that completes each sentence. The first one has been done for you.**

**1.** When Ann comes over, Dave is
_____**annoyed**_____ .

**2.** Jake and Dave were _____ Ann
of cake.

**3.** Ann said, "No, thanks! I pass. This is all your
_____ !"

**4.** Jake and Dave had made a _____ not
to like Ann.

**5.** The cake can't be _____ on Ann.

**6.** The cake made Jake look _____ .

**Write the answers to these questions. Use complete sentences.**

**7.** How were Jake and Dave depriving Ann?

_____

**8.** How is cake foisted on someone?

_____

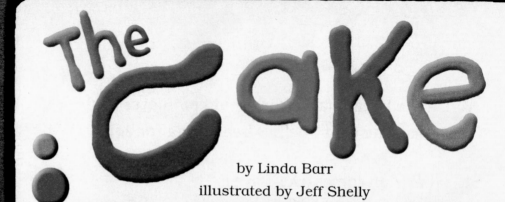

by Linda Barr

illustrated by Jeff Shelly

Dave is annoyed. Dave and Jake plan to have
a snack. Then Ann comes over. They had made a
pact not to like Ann.

Dave acts like he's glad to see her.

Then he looks at Jake. Jake *is* glad to see her!
What is this? Dave does not get it. **1**

## Stop and Think

**1** What do you know about Jake and Dave so far?

I know that Jake and Dave _____

_____

_____

# Game

"My dad baked a cake," Jake blabs to Ann. "He said we could have some. Look, take a plate!"

Ann looks at the cake. "Thanks! But no."

"I can take all that cake," Dave brags.

Jake grabs for the cake. "I'll have it!" **2**

## Stop and Think

**2** Why do you think Dave and Jake both want all the cake?

*I think they want all the cake because* _____

_____

_____

Jake and Dave take plates. They grab some cake.
Dave crams his cake down. Jake packs his cake in.
"I ate one," Dave brags. "Now I'll have two!"
Jake gags on some cake. Ann whacks him on the
back. "Not so fast, Jake!" **3**

**Stop and Think**

**3** What happens when Jake eats too fast?

When Jake eats too fast, he _____

_____

_____

© Harcourt

14

"That makes two for me!" Jake brags. Now he looks queasy.

Dave jabs at the cake on his plate. Then he looks over at Ann. "We are depriving Ann of cake, Jake."

Jake hands a plate to Ann. "Take some cake, Ann!" ④

**Stop and Think**

④ Do you think Ann will have some cake? Explain your answer.

I think Ann will _____

_____

_____

But the cake can't be foisted on Ann. "No, thanks! I pass. This is all your venture!"

Dave stares at Jake. Jake stares back. Then Dave has two, and so does Jake.

"The cake game is over," Dave states. "Could we save this for your dad?"  ❺

**Stop and Think**

❺ The cake game is over. Who wins? Explain your answer.

*When the cake game is over,* _____

_____

_____

Jake looks pale as he gazes at the cake. "I'll be glad to do that."

They take the cake in to Jake's dad. Then they scrape the scraps from their plates into a bag.

Ann pats Jake and Dave on the back. "I'm glad your cake game is over."

## Stop and Think

**6** How do you think Ann feels about the boys' cake game? What makes you think that?

I think Ann feels the cake game is _____

_____

Now Dave sees that Ann isn't so bad. "Do you like to skate?" Dave asks. "We go to a skate track on Grape Lane. You could come with Jake and me."

"OK. I can skate as fast as you two!" Ann brags. "We can go skate now!"

"Not now! We can't go fast now!" Jake gasps.

"Blame it on the cake!" says Ann. **7**

## Stop and Think

**7** Why does Ann say "Blame it on the cake"?

Ann says "Blame it on the cake" because _____

_____

_____

# Think Critically

**1.** What are the main events in the story? Copy the chart, and fill it in. **PLOT**

| Characters | Setting |
|---|---|

**Plot Events**
1. *Dave does not like Ann.*
2.
3.
4.

**2.** How do Dave's feelings about Ann change? **CHARACTER**

*In the beginning of the story, Dave* _____

_____

_____

*By the end of the story, Dave* _____

_____

_____

**3.** Why do you think the author chose not to have anyone win the cake game? **AUTHOR'S PURPOSE**

*I think the author did this because*

_____

_____

flinched

fluke

gaped

glared

legendary

muttered

snickering

stunned

# Vocabulary

## Build Robust Vocabulary

Read the selection and think about the meanings of the words in dark type.

When Danica Patrick came on the track, some people **gaped** at her. They giggled at her little size. They didn't see how she could win. "She is a kid," they **muttered.** "She can't win!" But Danica did win. They were **stunned.**

One man said it had to be a **fluke.** He didn't think she could win again. But she did. Some drivers who didn't win **glared** at Danica. She could have **flinched** when they glared, but she didn't. She didn't quit.

No one is **snickering** at Danica now. She is a **legendary** driver. All her fans go to the track to see her win.

**Write the Vocabulary Word that completes each sentence. The first one has been done for you.**

1. The drivers were amazed to see Danica on the track. Some _____gaped_____ at her.

2. Some drivers _____ at Danica. They didn't like to see her at the track.

3. Danica could have _____ when they looked at her like that, but she didn't. She didn't quit.

4. They _____ ,"She is a kid. She can't win!"

5. The drivers were _____ that Danica could win.

6. One man didn't think she could win again. He said one win could be a _____ .

7. Danica Patrick is a _____ driver. She has a lot of fans who come to see her win.

8. Some people giggled when Danica came on the track. But they are not _____ now.

# DRIVE

by Linda Barr

Danica Patrick is in the pit! She sits at the side of the track. She will get some gas as fast as she can. One man looks for rips in her tires. Danica still has miles and miles to drive.

Danica was driving even when she was a kid. Some gaped at her back then. "She is not a man," they muttered. "Look at her size. She can't do this. She can't win!" **1**

## Stop and Think

**1** Why did some people think Danica could not win?

*Some people thought Danica could not win because*

_____

_____

# FAST!

But Danica did win at times. When she didn't win, she still went quite fast. When she did win, the ones who didn't win glared at her. They were stunned that Danica could win. One man said it had to be a fluke.

That was a while back. No one is snickering now. They look for Danica. "Will she win?" they ask. They like to see her go so fast. **2**

## Stop and Think

**2** Some drivers snickered or glared at Danica. How would that make you feel?

*It would make me feel* _____

_____

23

In 2005, Danica was in the big one, the Indy 500. "She will drive as fast as the wind!" her fans said. "She will win!"

Fans were standing and waving at her as she passed. For a while, it looked as if she might win the Indy 500! Then Danica slid into a big pile-up on the track. She could have flinched and quit. But she didn't. **3**

## Stop and Think

**3** Do you think Danica will win this race? Explain your answer.

*I think Danica* _____

_____

_____

Her pit staff fixed her car. Danica could still drive! Danica was quick to get back on the track. She still could win. Drive fast, Danica!

Nine laps to go! Six laps to go!

But Danica could not take time out to get gas. As her tank ran out, she had to slip back. **4**

## Stop and Think

**4** What would happen if Danica stopped for gas?

*If Danica stopped for gas, then* _____

_____

_____

Danica didn't win the Indy 500. Still, what she did was legendary. Her fans had to smile and clap.

When Danica doesn't win, she still smiles. No one wins all the time. **5**

## Stop and Think

**5** The author says that what Danica did was *legendary*. Why does the author say this?

*The author says this because* _____

_____

When Danica isn't on the track, she visits sick kids. She visits classes. There, kids ask her, "When will you win a big one?"

Danica grins. She can drive fast. In time, she will win a big one. ❻

## Stop and Think

❻ Why do you think Danica knows she will win the big one some day?

*I think Danica knows she will win the big one some day because* _____

_____

Danica likes to be fit and trim. She skates for miles to get in shape.

Some ask Danica, "What if you could not drive?" Danica knows she would think of something. But for now she *can* drive.

Danica gets a big kick out of driving. At the same time, she and her staff do not look for fame. Danica just likes to win!

**Stop and Think**

7 Traits are words that describe people. What are some words that tell about Danica?

Danica is _____

_____

# Think Critically

1. Think about what Danica Patrick does. Copy the chart, and fill it in. **CHARACTER**

| Her Actions | Her Traits |
|---|---|
| drives fast wants to win helps kids | |

2. What is the main thing that this selection tells you about Danica Patrick? **MAIN IDEA AND DETAILS**

   *The main thing that this selection tells me about*

   *Danica Patrick is* _____

   _____

   _____

3. Why might Danica win a big race some day?
   **CAUSE AND EFFECT**

   *Danica might win a big race one day because*

   _____

   _____

© Harcourt

29

clusters

particular

sizzles

sparkling

stroll

surrender

# Vocabulary

## Build Robust Vocabulary

Write the Vocabulary Word that completes each sentence. The first one has been done for you.

Don's mom was driving him to camp. Mom said,

"Look!" There were **(1)** _____clusters_____ of

grass on fire. Don watched as smoke rose up from the

**(2)** _____ flames. He wished Rob

could be there to see it.

Rob had not gone to camp. Back at home, Rob met

a kid named Cole. Cole cracked bad jokes. Rob gave up.

He said, "Cole, I **(3)** _____ ! Stop!"

Rob missed Don.

One time, Rob went with Anna to

**(4)** _____ for a while and talk.

They didn't plan to do anything special. They

had no **(5)** _____ plans at all.

Don wrote a note to Rob. In his note,

he said, "Our camp is so hot. It

**(6)** _____ , and we

drip!" Don missed Rob.

**Write the answers to these questions. Use complete sentences.**

**7.** What are clusters of grass?

_____

_____

**8.** Who did Rob stroll with? Describe what they did.

_____

_____

# Clusters of Hope

by Luis Berrios

illustrated by Craig Orback

~~Donato~~ Don,
When will you come home?
I made a joke
as you drove off with your mom.
And then I spoke
of the big plans I'd do
without you.
Now I miss you a lot!
And that is not a joke.

I hope you like the camp.
And send a note to me.
~~Robert~~ Rob

## Stop and Think

**1** Why do you think Rob makes a joke when Don leaves for camp?

Rob makes a joke because _____

_____

_____

Rob,
    We rode for a while.
        Then Mom made a stop.
            She gave me a poke
            so I'd look.
        All I could see was fog, but
    Mom said, "That is smoke!"

    Clusters of grass were lit with
    sparkling fire.
        Smoke rose up from the flames.
            But without my pal to see it,
            it was not the same.

        I'm glad you are not mad.
        Send lots of notes to me.
Don 2

2 What do you know about Don and Rob so far?

I know that Don and Rob _____

_____

_____

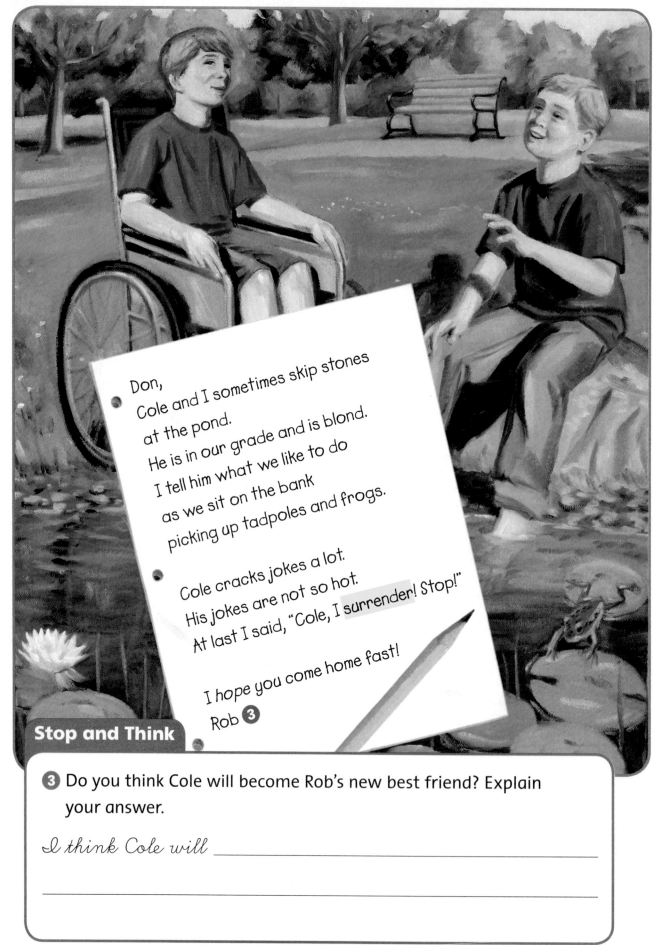

Don,
Cole and I sometimes skip stones at the pond.
He is in our grade and is blond.
I tell him what we like to do as we sit on the bank picking up tadpoles and frogs.

Cole cracks jokes a lot.
His jokes are not so hot.
At last I said, "Cole, I surrender! Stop!"

I hope you come home fast!
Rob ③

**Stop and Think**

③ Do you think Cole will become Rob's new best friend? Explain your answer.

I think Cole will _____

_____

Rob,
I spotted a lot of frogs.
We rode on a raft on the pond.
One time I ate five hot dogs.
But I did not get sick!

Did you get my note?
I can make one in code.
You can see it when I get home.

I hope you will still like my jokes!
Don **4**

## Stop and Think

**4** What do Rob and Don do that is the same?

Rob and Don both _____

_____

_____

Don,
Anna and I went to stroll for a while.
We had no particular plans at all.
Anna said, "What is in that hole?"
I smiled.
"A snake, but he is small!"

We went to get a snack.
All I had was a dime.
I didn't know what to do.
Anna said, "I'll get it this time."

I hope you come back fast!
Rob 5

## Stop and Think

5 Why do you think the author repeats the word *hope* in the notes?

I think he repeats the word because _____

_____

_____

Rob,
Our camp is so hot.
It sizzles, and we drip!
We named camp "The Hot Zone."
What a trip!

I take my fishing rod to the pond
And sit still on a stone.
I was glad to come to camp.
Now it's time to go home.

I hope you still have time for me!
Don ❻

## Stop and Think

❻ Don says "Now it's time to go home." What does he mean?

*When Don says "Now it's time to go home," he means*

_____

_____

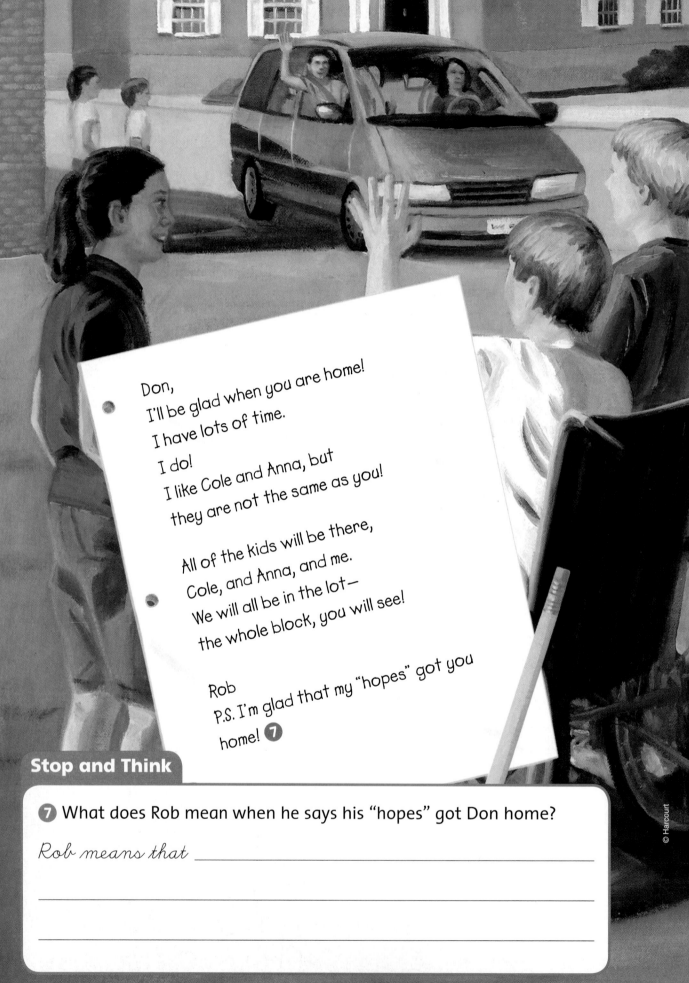

Don,
I'll be glad when you are home!
I have lots of time.
I do!
I like Cole and Anna, but
they are not the same as you!

All of the kids will be there,
Cole, and Anna, and me.
We will all be in the lot—
the whole block, you will see!

Rob
P.S. I'm glad that my "hopes" got you
home! ❼

## Stop and Think

❼ What does Rob mean when he says his "hopes" got Don home?

Rob means that _____

_____

_____

# Think Critically

**1.** What happens in the story? Copy the chart, and fill it in. **PLOT**

> **Plot Events**

**2.** What kind of friend do you think Rob would be? **CHARACTER**

*I think Rob would be the kind of friend who*

_____

_____

**3.** What message do you think the author wants you to understand from this poem? **THEME**

*I think the author wants me to* _____

_____

_____

| accusing |
| averted |
| craned |
| cringed |
| fury |
| interrogation |
| solemnly |
| stern |

# Vocabulary

## Build Robust Vocabulary

Read the story and think about the meanings of the words in dark type.

From the deck, Meg **craned** her neck to see. Their ship was about to land in the United States. When it landed, Meg and her mom got off the ship. Next, they had to pass **interrogation.** They had to pass some tests. Meg **cringed** when some men yelled, "Go fast!"

Meg and her mom got in line. A **stern** man sat near the end. When Meg got to him, he spoke to her **solemnly.** He asked, "Are you sick?" He gave her an **accusing** look.

In the next line, a man swelled with **fury.** His wife had not passed her tests. She had to go back home. Meg **averted** her gaze from the man and his wife.

Meg hoped to pass her tests. She wanted to live in the United States.

**Write the Vocabulary Word that completes each sentence. The first one has been done for you.**

1. Meg _____**craned**_____ her neck to see the United States.

2. Meg _____ when the men yelled at them.

3. Meg and her mom had to pass tests. They went to an _____ .

4. A man in the next line was mad. He swelled with _____ .

5. Meg _____ her gaze. She didn't look at the man and his wife.

6. At the testing spot, the man spoke to Meg _____ .

7. The _____ man asked Meg if she was sick.

8. He gave Meg an _____ look. Had she done something wrong?

# The BEST TIME

by Eva Ramos

Meg and her mom went up on the deck. Meg craned her neck to see. Their trip over the sea had lasted seven whole weeks. Now they were close to the United States.

But Meg and her mom were not quite there yet. They still had one stop to make. They had to pass interrogation. They had to pass some tests. **1**

## Stop and Think

**1** Where do you think Meg and her mom lived before?

*I think Meg and her mom* _____

_____

_____

The ship passed near the docks. Meg's dad had planned to meet them after the tests. She could see lots of men, but not her dad.

Meg's dad had come to the United States last year. He got a job and sent for them. At last, they were here! Now it was time for their interrogation. **2**

## Stop and Think

**2** How do you think Meg feels as she looks for her dad? Why?

*I think Meg feels* _____

_____

_____

At last, they landed. The testing site was made of red bricks. Its big top seemed to rise out of the sea. Meg stopped to look at it. But then men on the dock yelled, "Go fast!" Meg cringed. Mom grabbed her hand, and they ran.

Next, they went up lots of steps. Meg and her mom were tired and weak. But there was no time. They could rest when it was over. **3**

## Stop and Think

**3** Why are Meg and her mom tired and weak?

*Meg and her mom are tired and weak because* _____

_____

_____

At the big testing spot, Meg and her mom stopped. They had to stand in a line. A stern man sat near the end. When they got to him, he looked in Meg's ears. "Are you sick? How do you feel?" he asked. He gave her an accusing look.

"No, she is not the least bit sick," Mom said.

"I feel quite well!" Meg added. They had seen how the sick ones were sent back home. **4**

## Stop and Think

**4** How is Meg's test like the ones you take at school?

*Meg's test is like the ones I take at school because*

_____

_____

In the next line, a man passed his tests, but his wife did not. A test revealed that she had a disease. She had to go back home. The man swelled with fury. His wife sobbed. Meg stared. Then she remembered her manners and averted her gaze. Meg felt sad for them.

In the end, Meg and her mom passed all the tests. A man solemnly said that they were free to go into the United States! ⑤

## Stop and Think

⑤ Why does the author tell you about the husband and wife?

*The author tells me about the husband and wife* _____

_____

_____

Some did not pass the tests. They were sent home. Some were kept at the testing spot for weeks. Life was grim there. They screamed and begged. They asked to be let in. In the end, some of them were still sent home.

When Meg and her mom left the spot, they were so glad! Meg had tears on her cheeks. As they got near the docks, they could hear cheering. **6**

## Stop and Think

**6** Once Meg and her mom pass their tests, what do they do next?

*Once Meg and her mom pass their tests, they* _____

_____

_____

They had to look for Meg's dad. They kept at it for quite a while. Where was he? They had not seen him for more than a year!

Then Meg spotted him and yelled. She and her mom ran to greet him. There were many tears and smiles. At last, they were in the United States! This was the best time in Meg's life! **7**

## Stop and Think

**7** Do you think Meg will want to leave the United States and go back home? Explain your answer.

*I think Meg* _____

_____

# Think Critically

1. What happened in the story? Copy the chart, and fill it in.

   PLOT

   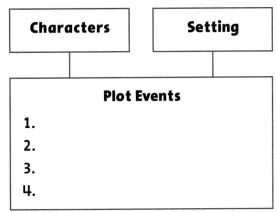

   | Characters | Setting |
   |---|---|

   **Plot Events**
   1.
   2.
   3.
   4.

2. What is the main idea of this story? **MAIN IDEA AND DETAILS**

   *The main idea of this story is* _____

   _____

   _____

3. Why do you think so many people tried to pass these tests? **MAKE INFERENCES**

   *I think many people tried to pass the tests so*

   *they* _____

   _____

   _____

# Vocabulary

## Build Robust Vocabulary

Write the word that best completes each sentence.
The first one has been done for you.

**1.** Ruben was sad. His mom could see that he felt

_____**downcast**_____ .

**extensive   culinary   downcast**

**2.** Ruben told his mom that Snack Week would be

_____ next week.

**depriving   commencing   foisting**

**3.** Ruben was _____ . "What snack

**legendary   pensive   reminiscent**

can I take to class?"

**4.** "It must be from my homeland. It needs to be

_____ of Cuba."

**reminiscent   downcast   pensive**

**5.** Ruben had a look of _____ .

**venture   consternation   clusters**

"Black beans do not sound fun," he said.

**6.** Ruben's pal Tucker likes to eat. The list of stuff he

likes to eat is _____ .

**extensive   downcast   sparkling**

**7.** "I ate _____ green frog's legs

**stern   pensive   vivid**

one time," said Ruben.

**8.** Mom said, "We could _____

**recruit   avert   annoy**

someone to help."

**9.** Mom smiled _____ as she

**queasily   serenely   solemnly**

said this.

**10.** "We will need someone with

_____ skills," said Ruben.

**downcast   culinary   vivid**

**Write the answers to these questions. Use complete
sentences.**

**11.** What has happened when something has commenced?

_____

**12.** If someone is pensive, what are they doing?

_____

# The FLAN PLAN

by Kathryn Powers • illustrated by Jana Christy

## CAST OF CHARACTERS

| Narrator | Ruben | Ruben's mom | Amanda |
|----------|-------|-------------|--------|
| Tucker | June | Chorus | |

**Narrator:** Ruben gets home. He feels downcast and looks at his feet. Mom sees this.

**Mom:** What is the problem, Ruben?

**Ruben:** In class, Mr. Hunt told us about Snack Week. He asked each of us to bring snacks to class.

**Chorus:** Yum! We like snacks.

**Mom:** That's not so bad!

**Ruben:** But Mr. Hunt has one rule. The snack must come from our homeland. **1**

**Stop and Think**

**1** What is another word for *downcast*? What is the opposite of *downcast*?

Another word for "downcast" is _____

The opposite of "downcast" is _____

52

**Mom:** I like that rule! When is this week commencing? Do we have some time to plan?

**Ruben:** That's the problem. It's next week!

**Mom:** Why are you so pensive, Ruben?

**Ruben:** I'm stumped! What snack could I take?

**Chorus:** Make it something fun!

**Mom:** We are from Cuba. Take a snack from there.

**Ruben:** Should I take a plate of black beans? No, beans do not sound fun.

**Narrator:** Amanda sees Ruben's look of consternation.

**Amanda:** What's the problem, Ruben? ❷

## Stop and Think

❷ **Why does Ruben think about taking black beans?**

Ruben thinks about taking black beans because _____

_____

_____

53

**Ruben:** I need to find a fun snack to take to class next week. It must come from my homeland.

**Amanda:** My dad makes a snack with cubes of fish and eggs. It comes from Japan, but you can use it.

**Chorus:** But Ruben is from Cuba, not Japan!

**Ruben:** Yes, I need a snack from *my* homeland.

**Narrator:** Then Tucker comes up.

**Tucker:** What's bugging you, Ruben? **3**

**Stop and Think**

**3** How are Ruben and Amanda the same?

*Ruben and Amanda are the same because* _____

_____

_____

**Amanda:** Ruben needs a snack to take to class next week. And he's stumped.

**Tucker:** Well, I have an extensive list of stuff I like to eat. I'd pick what I like best, hot dogs and buns!

**Chorus:** But the snack must come from Cuba!

**Tucker:** Well, don't they eat hot dogs in Cuba, Ruben?

**Ruben:** Yes, but . . .

**Chorus:** Tell them some real snacks from Cuba! ❹

## Stop and Think

❹ How would you describe Amanda?

*Amanda is* _____

_____

_____

© Harcourt

55

**Ruben:** Well, I ate vivid green frog's legs one time.

**Narrator:** Ruben says this with a big grin.

**Tucker:** You didn't!

**Ruben:** I'm kidding, Tucker! Besides, frog's legs are not a snack from Cuba.

**Narrator:** Then June comes up to them.

**June:** What's up? You all look puzzled.

**Chorus:** Ruben needs a snack from Cuba! **5**

**5** Is Ruben really thinking about taking frog's legs? Explain your answer.

*Ruben is* _____

_____

_____

**June:** I could take my grandma's pumpkin cakes.

**Chorus:** Cakes made out of pumpkin?

**June:** Yes! They are sweet.

**Ruben:** Mom, what do they eat in Cuba?

**Narrator:** Mom thinks about this a bit. Then she smiles.

**Mom:** Well, they do eat flan.

**Ruben:** Flan! That's it! I'll take that for a snack! **6**

## Stop and Think

**6** How can you tell Ruben knows what flan is?

*I can tell Ruben knows what flan is because* _____

_____

_____

57

**Chorus:** What's that? Is it just like cake?

**Mom:** No, but you do use milk and eggs to make it. It's so reminiscent of Cuba. Let's recruit Grandma to help us make it, Ruben.

**Tucker:** Could you make two? One for his class and one for us?

**Narrator:** Mom smiles serenely as she nods.

**Mom:** Yes, that's a grand culinary plan.

**Ruben:** It will be our flan plan! ➐

### Stop and Think

➐ How are flan and cake the same?

*Here is how they are the same:* _____

_____

_____

© Harcourt

58

# Think Critically

**1.** Ruben's teacher says that the snacks must come from the students' homeland. Why does Ruben's mom like that rule?
**CHARACTER**

*Ruben's mom likes that rule because* _____

_____

_____

**2.** Do you think the class will like Ruben's snack? Explain your answer. **MAKE PREDICTIONS**

*I think the class will* _____

_____

_____

**3.** Sometimes authors have two purposes for writing. What are two purposes for this play? **AUTHOR'S PURPOSE**

*Two purposes the author might have had to write*

*this play are* _____

_____

_____

attentive

contradicting

darted

jostling

pounced

responsible

swerved

# Vocabulary

## Build Robust Vocabulary

Write the Vocabulary Word that completes each sentence. The first one has been done for you.

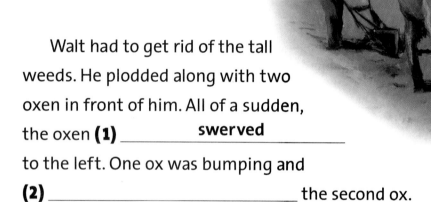

Walt had to get rid of the tall weeds. He plodded along with two oxen in front of him. All of a sudden, the oxen **(1)** _____swerved_____ to the left. One ox was bumping and **(2)** _____ the second ox.

Walt was hot and tired, but he did his job well. He was a **(3)** _____ lad. He walked up to see what was upsetting the oxen. Walt gasped as a rattlesnake **(4)** _____ near him.

© Harcourt

Then Dad came over. The snake was gone. Dad said, "You must be (5) _____ , Walt. You must look out for snakes."

Walt thought to himself, *I will not be*

(6) _____ *Dad about that!*

Later, Dad told Walt that he used to have a cat named Jude. One time, Jude had jumped on top of a rattlesnake. Dad said Jude was brave. "He

(7) _____ on that snake!"

**Write the answers to these questions. Use complete sentences.**

**8.** How did one ox jostle the other one? Describe what was happening.

_____

_____

**9.** What would Walt be doing if he was contradicting his dad?

_____

_____

# CLOSE CALL

by Pam Barrett • illustrated by Adam Gustavson

Walt plodded along. He felt hot and tired. Still, he was a responsible lad. It was his job to get rid of the tall weeds.

All of a sudden, one ox halted, peered at its feet, and grunted. Then it bumped and jostled the second ox.

"Calm down," Walt called out. "Get along."

Then the two oxen swerved. Walt walked up to see what was upsetting them. When he looked down, he gasped. **1**

## Stop and Think

**1** What do you think is upsetting the oxen?

I think the oxen are upset by _____

_____

_____

A snake darted near him! "Dad!" Walt called. "I need help! It's a rattlesnake!"

His dad ran over and froze near Walt. "Be still, Walt. If you do not scare a snake, it will leave."

"I think it left, Dad."

"You must be attentive, Walt," Dad stated. "A snake is just as scared of you as you are of it. If you hear a rattle, that is a signal. The snake is telling you, 'Leave me alone. Go back.'"

Walt nodded. "That was a close call." ②

**Stop and Think**

② **Where do you think the story takes place? Explain.**

*I think the story takes place* _____

_____

_____

© Harcourt

After their meal, Dad had a tale to tell Walt. "When I was a lad, I had a cat named Jude. He was the size of a dog! And Jude was brave.

"One time Jude had a big rattlesnake backed into a spot near the animal pen. Jude was hissing, and the snake was rattling. All of a sudden, Jude pounced on that snake. Held it fast."

"Did you kill the snake, Dad?"

"I didn't have to. Jude did it for me. I want you to see this, Walt." ❸

## Stop and Think

❸ What do you think Walt's dad wants him to see?

*I think Walt's dad wants him to see* _____

_____

_____

Dad walked over to a shelf and picked up a small box. Inside, it held the rattle end of a rattlesnake.

"Was this from the snake Jude got?" Walt asked.

"It was. I kept it for luck, so snakes would leave me alone. Now I want you to have it."

Walt just stared at the rattle in the box. He didn't want to run into a snake that big at all! ❹

**Stop and Think**

❹ A snake's rattle will bring you good luck. Is this statement a fact or an opinion? Explain.

*This statement is* _____

_____

Walt cleaned up for bedtime. He peeked at the rattle one last time and set the box near his bed.

For a while, Walt could not fall asleep. When he did at last, he dreamed. In his dream, he could hear the snake, *rattle, rattle, rattle*. Walt woke up. But he could still hear it.

*Rattle, rattle, rattle.*

Was a snake near his bed? **5**

## Stop and Think

**5** Why do you think Walt has trouble falling asleep?

*I think Walt has trouble falling asleep because* _____

_____

_____

Walt rolled up in a ball. He wanted to call for his mom and dad but he felt stiff with fear.

Then, at last, Walt yelled, "Dad, I hear a big snake!"

"There is no snake, Walt," Dad called. "Calm down. It's just a dream. You will fall back to sleep in a bit!"

*Rattle, rattle, rattle.*

"Dad, I don't mean to be contradicting you. But I *do* hear a big snake!" Walt called back. **6**

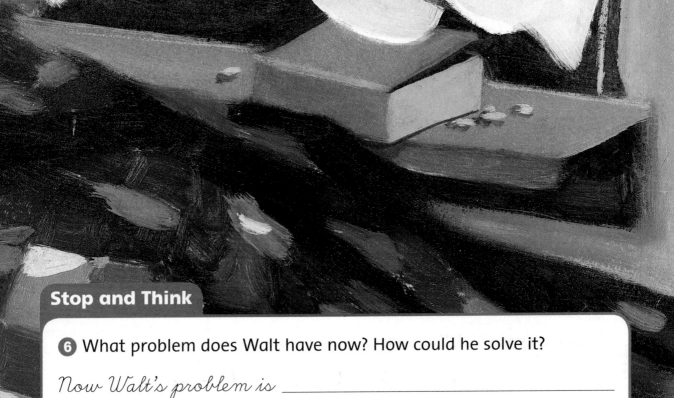

## Stop and Think

**6** What problem does Walt have now? How could he solve it?

*Now Walt's problem is* _____

_____

_____

At last his dad came to look. He looked in and grinned. "The wind comes in," Dad said. "That makes the rattle roll in the box. That's what you hear."

"There is no big snake?" Walt asked.

Dad smiled and said, "No snake."

Walt smiled back. "That felt like a close call."

Dad nodded. "That's it for close calls." He went back down the hall.

Walt peeked one last time at the rattle. Then he tucked in his blanket and fell back asleep. **7**

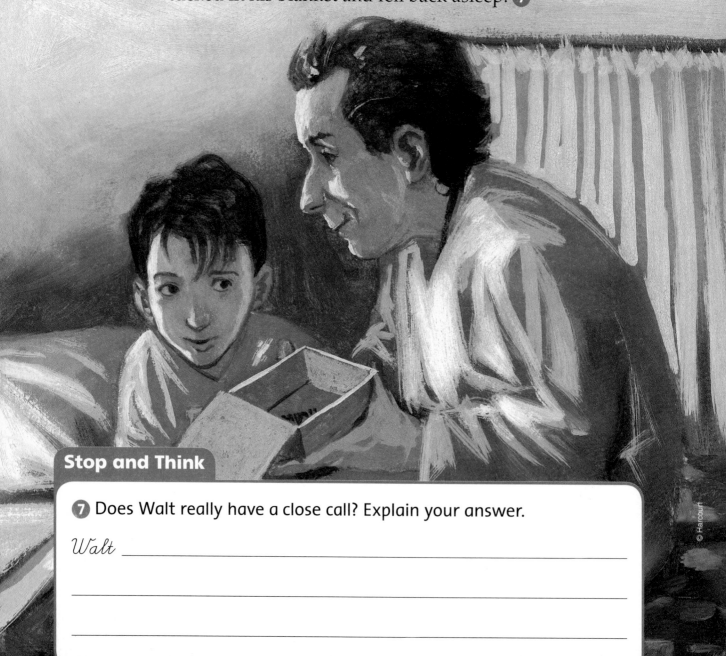

**Stop and Think**

**7** Does Walt really have a close call? Explain your answer.

Walt _____

_____

_____

# Think Critically

1. What happened in the story? Copy the chart, and fill it in. **PLOT**

   | Plot Events |
   | --- |
   | 1. *Walt has a close call with a rattlesnake.* |
   | 2. |
   | 3. |
   | 4. |

2. Why does Walt dream about a snake? **CAUSE AND EFFECT**

   *Walt dreams about a snake because* _____

   _____

   _____

3. The author tells a story but also includes information about rattlesnakes. Why do you think the author included this information? **AUTHOR'S PURPOSE**

   *The author included this information* _____

   _____

   _____

inspecting

lurked

reluctant

resounded

rumpled

surge

taut

untangled

### Build Robust Vocabulary

Read the story and think about the meanings of the words in dark type.

Jay's grandma wanted to send a note to someone. She seemed **reluctant** to use e-mail. "E-mail is just for kids," she said.

Jay **untangled** the **rumpled** wires and plugged in the cord. He made sure the wires were not pulled **taut**. Grandma was **inspecting** the screen when it blinked. She jumped. Grandma acted like something bad **lurked** inside the laptop.

"Here, let me," said Jay. Then Jay clicked some keys. The clicking keys **resounded** in the den. Then words popped up on the screen.

"How did you do that?" Grandma asked. Jay felt a **surge** of pride.

**Write the Vocabulary Word that completes each sentence. The first one has been done for you.**

1. Grandma acted like something bad
_____**lurked**_____ inside the laptop.

2. Jay's grandma was _____ to use
e-mail to send a note.

3. The laptop wires were a _____
mess. Jay fixed that.

4. Jay's grandma was looking at the laptop. She was
_____ it.

5. Jay _____ all the wires and
plugged in the cord.

6. Jay made sure the wires were not pulled
_____ .

7. Jay felt a _____ of pride.

8. The clicking keys _____ in the den.

# You Have Mail!

**by Amber Anderson**

**illustrated by Amy Wummer**

"Will you drive me over to the mall now?" Jay asked. "I picked up all my stuff like you asked."

But his grandma sat down at her desk. She got out a pad and a pen. "Just wait," she said. "I need to send a note to Gail. It will not take long."

Jay had hoped for a fast trip to the mall. He had cut grass for a man down the street. Jay had saved a lot of his pay, but he wanted to spend some, too. **1**

## Stop and Think

**1** How do you think Jay felt when his grandma sat down to write her letter? Why?

*I think Jay felt* _____

_____

"You could send an e-mail," Jay said. "Your note is called 'snail mail.' It will take days. E-mail is fast!"

Grandma nodded. "So you say. But I like to use 'snail mail.' E-mail is just for kids."

"What if I help you?" Jay asked. "Gail can read it the same day it's sent!"

Grandma had stopped, but she seemed reluctant.

"Grandma!" Jay added. "Gail can read it the same day it's sent!"

## Stop and Think

**2** Why do you think Grandma says e-mail is just for kids?

*I think Grandma says e-mail is just for kids because*

_____

_____

"We will take it one step at a time," Jay begged.
He grabbed Dad's laptop.

"Wait!" Grandma said.

"It's okay! Dad lets me use this." Jay untangled
and plugged in the cord. He made sure it was not
pulled taut. Then he flipped the laptop on.

Grandma was inspecting the screen when it
blinked. She jumped back. Jay smiled. ❸

## Stop and Think

❸ Why does Grandma say "Wait"?

Grandma says "Wait" because _____

_____

_____

©Harcourt

But Grandma didn't smile. Jay could see she was not at all sure about this. She acted like something bad lurked inside the laptop. She pushed her chair back.

Jay said, "Wait, Grandma! You can do this!" He clicked some keys. "Dear Gail" popped up.

Grandma smiled. "How did you do that?" ❹

Dear Gail,

© Harcourt

**Stop and Think**

❹ What problem does Jay have?

*Jay's problem is* _____

_____

_____

75

In no time, Grandma was at it. Her clicking keys resounded in the small den.

When she stopped, she peeked at Jay. "That's the end of my note. Did Gail get it yet?"

Jay smiled. "Not yet. Now you have to send your note."

But Grandma didn't have the e-mail address. She had to call Gail. **5**

## Stop and Think

**5** Why doesn't Grandma have Gail's e-mail address?

*Grandma doesn't have Gail's e-mail address because*

_____

_____

Grandma said to Gail, "Is your laptop on? Just keep it on! You will be amazed."

Grandma hung up. Jay added Gail's address to the e-mail. He had Grandma press the "send" key.

"I did it!" Grandma said with a surge of pride. Then she grabbed the note on her desk. She wadded it up and tossed the rumpled note aside. ❻

## Stop and Think

❻ Do you think Grandma will use only e-mail from now on? Explain.

I think Grandma _____

_____

_____

Grandma said, "I like to write notes, but I can use e-mail as well! Can I use the laptop, Jay? I have notes to send!"

"Yes, but can we go to the mall?" Jay asked. "I want to spend some of my pay. And we can look for a laptop for you!"

Grandma grinned. "Okay. I like that plan!"

Then the screen blinked. "You have mail!" Jay and Grandma smiled all the way to the mall. **7**

### Stop and Think

**7** What does this story teach you?

*This story teaches me that* _____

_____

_____

# Think Critically

**1.** Think about the problems in the story. How was each problem solved? Copy the chart, and fill it in.

CONFLICT/RESOLUTION

| Jay's Problem | Grandma's Problem |
|:---:|:---:|
| ↓ | ↓ |
| Solution | Solution |

**2.** How do Grandma's feelings change? **MAKE COMPARISONS**

In the beginning, Grandma _____

_____

At the end, Grandma _____

_____

**3.** Why does Jay smile at the end? **CAUSE AND EFFECT**

Jay smiles because _____

_____

_____

cease

exist

fierce

impressed

nimble

slick

# Vocabulary

## Build Robust Vocabulary

Write the Vocabulary Word that completes each sentence in the news articles. The first one has been done for you.

DAILY NEWS                    SECTION C

# Homes Under Attack

by Anna G. Smith                              Friday, June 10

Nearby homes have been smashed. No one is sure how this happened. Niles Pig said, "One moment my home was there. Then it was gone! My straw home didn't cost much, but it looked

**(1)** _____slick_____ ."

The home of Max Pig was smashed, too. It's gone now. It doesn't **(2)** _____ any longer. "I am very unhappy," said Max. "First a tree fell on my truck. Now, this happens! My problems will never **(3)** _____ ." Some think that a **(4)** _____ wind smashed the homes.

# Wolf Seen Around Smashed Homes

by Anna G. Smith                              Friday, June 17

Last week, two nearby homes
were smashed. Hazel Pig stated
that a big wolf is to blame. "I
witnessed the whole thing.
I yelled at the wolf, but he
ran away. He was very fast and

**(5)** _____ ," said Hazel.

"I was very **(6)** _____ by his speed,"
she added. She went on to say that she plans to help
Niles and Max. "They have no place to live now."

# The Pigs, the Wolf, and a Laptop

by Pamela K. Jennett • illustrated by Chris Lensch

## Cast of Characters

**Narrator**     **Milton**     **Max**     **Niles**     **Hazel**

**NARRATOR:** There were three little pigs. Each had a home. Then along came a wolf. Now just one home stands.

**MILTON:** Little pigs, you can't stay in that brick home forever. I'll be back. (*Exits to the right.*)

**MAX:** What will we do?

**HAZEL:** (*To Niles.*) Why did you make your home out of straw? (*To Max.*) Why did you pick sticks?

**NILES and MAX:** They didn't cost much!

**HAZEL:** And they can't keep the wolf out. ❶

## Stop and Think

❶ Why did Niles and Max make their homes with straw and sticks?

*They made their homes with straw and sticks because*

_____

_____

**NILES:** Why did you pick bricks?

**HAZEL:** I used my laptop. Watch. I type what I want, and the laptop finds it.

**NILES and MAX:** Can you help us?

**NARRATOR:** Hazel types *straw homes,* and a list of websites pops up. She reads the list carefully.

**NILES:** (*Amazed.*) These are homes made from bundles of straw.

**HAZEL:** The bundles make the walls strong.

**NILES:** I'm impressed. I didn't think of putting the straw in bundles.

**NARRATOR:** Next, Hazel types *stick homes.*

**HAZEL:** Those sticks are logs. A wolf can't blow down a log home! **2**

**Stop and Think**

**2** What other things might Hazel look for on her laptop to help Niles and Max?

*Hazel could look for* _____

_____

**HAZEL:** Websites can be very helpful. Some will have things you need. Some websites look slick, but they don't tell you much. You must pick carefully.

**NILES:** Let's type *wolf homes,* and see what we get.

**NARRATOR:** Hazel types on the keys again.

**MAX:** Do you think Milton has seen this?

**HAZEL:** It says that this is where wolves exist now. It's called Alaska.

**MAX:** You mean Milton isn't supposed to be *here?* ❸

## Stop and Think

❸ What do you think will happen next?

*I think that* _____

_____

_____

**NILES:** We can help him. He won't expect that!

**HAZEL:** Yes. Milton is a long way from home, it seems.

**MAX:** I'm not sure he needs our help.

**HAZEL:** Let's help *you*! I'll print out these steps. Quick! We don't have much time.

**NARRATOR:** The pigs rush to finish the two new homes. **4**

## Stop and Think

**4** How do the pigs find out how to build better homes?

*The pigs find out how to build better homes by* _____

_____

_____

**MILTON:** I'm back! *(He huffs and puffs.)*

**HAZEL:** Cease that huffing and puffing.

**NARRATOR:** The new homes would not blow down.

**MILTON:** Oh, no! No one will think I am fierce now.

**NARRATOR:** The pigs have never seen the wolf act like this. They don't know what to think.

**MAX:** *(Whispering.)* Will Milton go away now?

**NILES:** I feel bad for Milton.

**HAZEL:** Milton, we think we can help you!

**NILES:** But you must promise to leave us alone. **5**

### Stop and Think

**5** What happens after Milton finds he cannot blow the houses down?

*After Milton finds he cannot blow the houses down,*

**MAX:** No huffing or puffing. No biting or scratching.

**MILTON:** I promise. I do! How can you help me?

**NILES:** Watch this.

**NARRATOR:** Hazel's nimble little feet type on the laptop keys. The wolf website appears.

**MILTON:** Hey! They look just like me! But where is this spot? Look at all of those trees!

**NILES:** That is Alaska. I think you may like it there.

**MAX:** It's your real home. You can be with the rest of the wolves. **6**

**Stop and Think**

**6** Do you think Milton will leave the pigs alone? Explain.

*I think that Milton* _____

_____

_____

**MILTON:** What a splendid plan. Yes, that's what I will do. How can I thank you?

**MAX:** Well, stop blowing down our homes.

**HAZEL:** If you like Alaska, *that* will make us happy.

**NARRATOR:** So the wolf set off for Alaska. The pigs settled in their new homes, as safe as can be. Now when they have a problem, they check what to do on the laptop. **7**

## Stop and Think

**7** Did the author write this play to entertain you or to teach you something? Explain your answer.

*I think the author wrote this play to* _____

_____

# Think Critically

**1.** What happens in the story? Copy the chart, and fill it in. **PLOT**

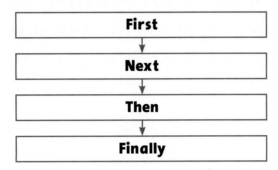

| First |
| --- |
| Next |
| Then |
| Finally |

**2.** How is Niles' second home different from his first one? How is it the same? **COMPARE AND CONTRAST**

*This is how it is different:* _____

_____

*This is how it is the same:* _____

_____

**3.** Why do the pigs want to help Milton? **CHARACTERS**

*The pigs want to help Milton because* _____

_____

_____

bond

delicate

flexible

infest

inspires

intervals

preserve

unique

# Vocabulary

## Build Robust Vocabulary

Write the Vocabulary Word that completes each sentence in the letters. The first one has been done for you.

Dear Shane,

Next week, Mom and Dad will help raise a new barn. I'll get to see it all!

In the past five years, Mr. Hall's barn started to sag. Bugs began to **(1)** _____infest_____ it. The barn is no longer safe. No one can **(2)** _____ it, so it must be taken down. A new barn will be raised in the same spot.

Mr. Hall said that not all barn raisings are the same. Each barn is **(3)** _____ . I wish you could be here to see it with me!

Your pal,
Chelsea

Dear Shane,

It's lunchtime on the day of the barn raising. The wall frames are up! Next, the team will build the top of the barn. They will lay long planks on top of the frames. The planks are **(4)** _____ , but if they bend too much, they can crack. Getting them up there will be a **(5)** _____ job. The team must make sure that the planks do not get broken.

The next time you visit, you will see the new barn!

Your pal,
Chelsea

Dear Shane,

Raising a barn is hard work! Dad had to make sure the gaps between the wall planks were the same. Then the team attached the wall planks at marked **(6)** _____ . The barn was finished in no time!

The people on the team now have a strong **(7)** _____ . It will bring them together to raise the next barn. Watching a barn raising **(8)** _____ me to do the same some day. Maybe you can do it with me!

Your pal,
Chelsea

# Raising a Barn

**by Linda Barr • illustrated by Stacey Schuett**

You can raise chickens, you can raise a garden, but how do you raise a barn? In the past, all barns were raised by hand. Often, a barn was raised in one day. People still raise barns, but now hard hats keep them safe!

A farm may have a barn that is in such bad shape that no one can preserve it. It starts to sag, and bugs infest it. Then it must be taken down. ❶

## Stop and Think

❶ Why might a barn need to be replaced?

*A barn might need to be replaced when* _____

_____

_____

A new barn will be raised. People come from all over to help. Over one hundred volunteers may help raise a single barn!

To start, the old planks are carted away. Some trees on the farm may be cut for the barn. Poplar trees are best. Sometimes, a farmer might trade crops or animals to get part of what is needed to build the barn. ❷

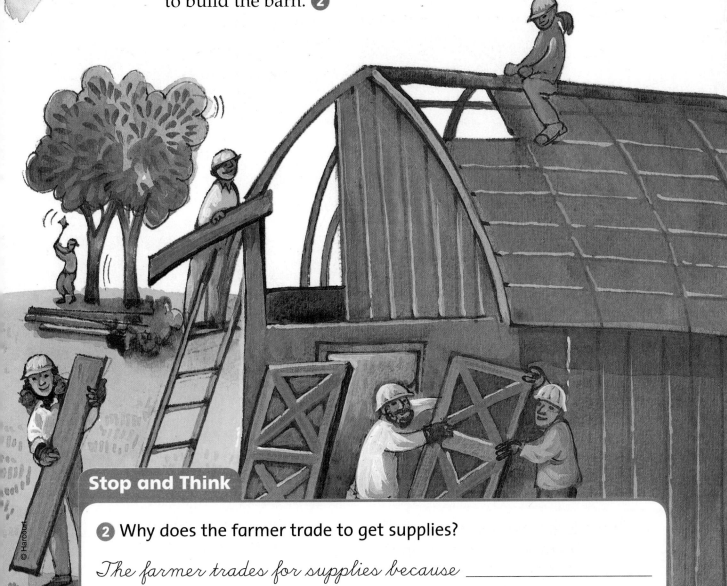

**Stop and Think**

❷ Why does the farmer trade to get supplies?

*The farmer trades for supplies because* _____

_____

_____

Then cars and trucks arrive at the farm. People prepare to start. A lot of them have helped to build barns in the past.

Some people help build the barn. Others do their part by fixing lunch. The children stay out of harm's way as they stand and watch. Some day, they may help raise a barn! **3**

## Stop and Think

**3** Small children cannot help raise the barn. Why do their parents bring them to the barn raising?

Parents bring them because_____

_____

_____

Big stones or blocks will make the base of the barn. Then a frame is made for each wall. Sometimes, the team uses nails. Sometimes, they use sharp pegs carved from trees.

Now is the time to "raise" the barn! The people use their arms to lift one frame up as far as they can. Then, some of the team presses on the frame with long poles. **4**

## Stop and Think

**4** Why do they call this "raising" a barn?

*They call this "raising" a barn because* _____

_____

_____

© Harcourt

Each frame is raised in the same way. It's hard, but the barn is starting to take shape!

To build the top, long planks are laid on each frame. Getting each of these up there is a delicate job. The long planks are somewhat flexible. But if they flex too much, they can crack. Some people stand on top of the frame. Those with strong arms lift the planks up. The planks fit into slots in the frame, as if they are parts to a puzzle. When they fit well, the planks cannot shift. **5**

## Stop and Think

**5** Why is moving the planks to the top a delicate job?

*Moving the planks to the top is a delicate job because*

_____

_____

Then, the team completes the top of the barn. Sometimes, the top is flat. On some barns, it is shaped. Each barn is unique! When all the parts are nailed down, the top will be quite strong.

Next, the team starts nailing planks to the wall frames. Each is attached at marked intervals. In no time, the walls are finished. **6**

## Stop and Think

**6** What would happen if the intervals on the frame were not marked?

*If the intervals were not marked,* _____

_____

_____

At last, it's time to rest and eat. But soon, the people get back to work. It's getting dark when the last part is nailed down. The barn is finished.

The tired people walk to their cars and trucks. They are smiling. They have a bond that brings them back to raise the next barn. They hope that watching them raise barns inspires their children to do the same some day. ⑦

## Stop and Think

⑦ How does the author show you that barn raising is hard work?

The author _____

_____

_____

# Think Critically

**1.** How did the author show you that barn raising is fun?
Copy the chart, and fill it in. **AUTHOR'S PURPOSE**

| Author's Purpose | Author's Perspective | Evidence |
|---|---|---|
| to persuade | Barn raising is fun. | |

**2.** How do most people learn how to raise a barn? **DRAW CONCLUSIONS**

*Most people learn how to raise a barn when they*

_____

_____

**3.** Why do people still raise barns by hand? **MAKE INFERENCES**

*People still raise barns by hand because*

_____

_____

_____

# Vocabulary

## Build Robust Vocabulary

Write the word that best completes each sentence.
The first one has been done for you.

1. Joan is _____exuberant_____ when Justin

   **flexible   rumpled   exuberant**

   asks her to go with him on a hike. Joan likes
   hiking!

2. On their hike, Justin and Joan stop to look. They

   _____ the hills.

   **scan   cease   exist**

3. They see a big bird land on a branch. The

   _____ branch bobs up

   **unique   pliable   fierce**

   and down under the big bird.

4. They see an eagle chick. It fell from its nest. The

   chick is weak and _____ .

   **flexible   nimble   vulnerable**

5. The chick's mom and dad must feed and

   _____ the chick so it can grow.

   **infest   nurture   scan**

**6.** An adult eagle can _____ a chick

                **encircle  exist  pounce**

with its wings to keep it from harm.

**7.** It's bad for an eagle chick to be alone and

_____ .

**taut  pliable  solitary**

**8.** If a big animal _____ near,

            **scans  lumbers  inspires**

the chick may not be safe.

**9.** When the eagle chick is _____ ,

            **mature  exuberant  slick**

it will be safe on its own.

**10.** Joan and Justin can't _____ why

          **lumber  cease  comprehend**

the chick was left on its own.

**Write the answers to these questions. Use complete sentences.**

**11.** How do you act when you are exuberant?

_____

**12.** If something is pliable, what is it like?

_____

# Joan's Eagle

by Kathryn Powers

illustrated by Tuesday Mourning

## Characters

| | | |
|---|---|---|
| **Narrator** | **Chorus** | **Joan** |
| **Kit** | **Rob** | **Justin** |

**Narrator:** Justin asks Joan to go on a hike. Joan is exuberant about Justin's plan. She can't wait!

**Justin:** Just tell me when you get tired, Joan. I'll slow down.

**Joan:** Don't slow down for me!

**Justin:** We'll be on a path, so no moaning and groaning.

**Joan:** Not me! I can do it.

**Chorus:** We think Joan may moan and groan! ❶

## Stop and Think

❶ Why do you think Justin expects Joan to moan and groan?

*I think Justin expects Joan to moan and groan because*

_____

_____

**Narrator:** Sometimes Joan just can't help but brag.

**Joan:** Today, I want to spot an eagle! I'll spot a dozen! Maybe I'll show you one.

**Justin:** Don't be upset if we spot nothing but trees.

**Joan:** Nothing but trees? Not on *my* hike!

**Narrator:** Justin smiles. He's used to Joan and her boasting. But he hopes she gets to see an eagle. ❷

**Stop and Think**

❷ Why does Justin think Joan might be upset?

*Justin thinks Joan might be upset because* _____

_____

_____

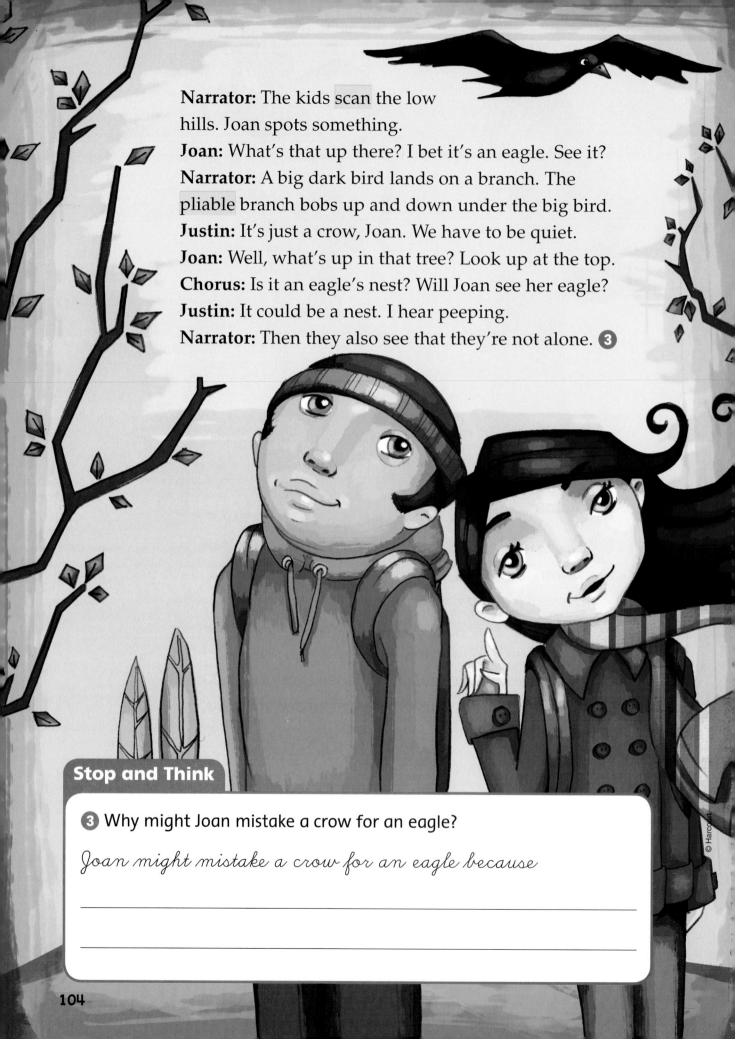

**Narrator:** The kids scan the low hills. Joan spots something.

**Joan:** What's that up there? I bet it's an eagle. See it?

**Narrator:** A big dark bird lands on a branch. The pliable branch bobs up and down under the big bird.

**Justin:** It's just a crow, Joan. We have to be quiet.

**Joan:** Well, what's up in that tree? Look up at the top.

**Chorus:** Is it an eagle's nest? Will Joan see her eagle?

**Justin:** It could be a nest. I hear peeping.

**Narrator:** Then they also see that they're not alone. ❸

**Stop and Think**

❸ Why might Joan mistake a crow for an eagle?

*Joan might mistake a crow for an eagle because*

_____

_____

**Kit:** Kids, stay low! You'll scare it!

**Chorus:** Scare what? What is it?

**Rob:** A little eagle fell out of its nest.

**Kit:** We're Rob and Kit Snow. We watch the eagles all of the time. But today, this chick needs help.

**Joan:** There it is, all fuzzy and cute!

**Kit:** It's quite vulnerable now. This eagle needs its mom and dad to feed and nurture it, so it grows. ❹

## Stop and Think

❹ **What do you think will happen to the baby eagle?**

*I think the baby eagle will* _____

_____

_____

**Narrator:** The kids bend low to look.

**Chorus:** Where are the mom and dad?

**Kit:** They seem to have flown away. I can't comprehend why they left a chick on its own. I have watched eagles encircle chicks with their wings to keep them safe.

**Justin:** But it's solitary now, all alone.

**Joan:** Do you think the mom and dad will show up?

**Rob:** I hope so. Still, if they *do* fly back, they can't get the chick up into the nest. **5**

## Stop and Think

**5** What would you do if you found a baby animal alone and in danger? Why?

I would _____

_____

_____

**Narrator:** Joan can't leave a little eagle on its own!

**Joan:** What if a big animal lumbers near? I'll tuck the eagle in my coat and take it home.

**Kit and Rob:** No! Don't do that!

**Joan:** Why not? I'll keep it safe until it's grown. **6**

## Stop and Think

**6** Does Joan have a good solution to the chick's problem? How can you tell?

Joan _____

_____

**Kit:** That's not best for the eagle, Joan. We'll take it to a man at the animal park.

**Rob:** He takes care of eagles until they are mature. Then the eagles can be on their own.

**Narrator:** Joan can't wait to get home.

**Joan:** Wait until I tell Mom and Dad I helped a baby eagle!

**Chorus:** You will not be bragging this time, Joan! **7**

**Stop and Think**

**7** Do you think Justin is sorry he took Joan on the hike with him? Explain your answer.

I think Justin _____

_____

# Think Critically

**1.** How do you think the author feels about people trying to take care of eagles on their own? **AUTHOR'S PURPOSE**

*I think the author feels* _____

_____

_____

**2.** Think about Joan's problem at the beginning of the story. How is the problem solved? **CONFLICT/RESOLUTION**

*Joan's problem is solved when* _____

_____

_____

**3.** What useful information does the author tell you about eagles? **MAKE INFERENCES**

*The author tells me* _____

_____

_____

avoid

deceptive

lure

mimics

obvious

predators

resemble

traits

# Vocabulary

## Build Robust Vocabulary

Write the Vocabulary Word that completes each sentence in the diary. The first one has been done for you.

Monday

    Today in class, we looked at a film. We got to see what it's like for animals that live in the Arctic. It's quite cold there. For part of the year, it stays dark all the time.

    How can animals stay alive in the Arctic? Some have white coats. They are safe and hard to see because they **(1)** _____resemble_____ the snow. That makes it hard for **(2)** _____ to hunt them. Some animals sleep away the winter to **(3)** _____ the freezing cold. These **(4)** _____ help animals stay alive in the Arctic.

© Harcourt

For the coldest part of the year, the Arctic fox is white. What happens when the snow melts? A white animal would be

(5) _____ , wouldn't it? You could see it plain as day! Well, get this! For part of the year, the Arctic fox is gray. The fox's gray coat (6) _____ the look of melting snow. This helps the fox sneak up on little animals and catch them. If they can't see the fox, it can

(7) _____ them from their dens—and eat them! Incredible!

If I ever get to go to the Arctic, now I'll know to look out! Seeing nothing but white in the Arctic can be

(8) _____ .

# BORN FOR SNOW

### by Linda Barr

How cold is cold? The animals up in the far north, or Arctic, can tell you. The Arctic is near the North Pole. The air there can be less than 30 degrees below zero. Strong winds roar. Storms drop thick blankets of snow.

The days are quite short. For part of the year, it stays dark for weeks at a time. You will not see trees or plants, just snow and more snow. ❶

## Stop and Think

❶ What do you think you will learn about the animals that live in the Arctic?

*I think I will learn* _____

_____

_____

Then spring comes to some parts of the Arctic. It's still cold, but not as much. The snow melts a little. Grass and small plants grow. Animals find more to eat.

In a short time, fall will bring more snow. Then there will be little for the animals to eat.

How do animals stay alive here? They are born with traits that help them. Some just avoid the cold. They find caves and snore away the coldest part of the year. **2**

## Stop and Think

**2** Why do some Arctic animals sleep through the coldest months?

*Some Arctic animals sleep through the coldest months because*

_____

_____

# LEMMING

Lemmings are little animals. When it gets too cold, they dig tunnels in the snow and stay there. The thick snow keeps out some of the cold. Plus, it hides the lemmings from animals who want them for a quick meal.

# WALRUS

Some animals in the far north are like the walrus. A walrus can store up fat, or blubber. It can store up six inches or more of fat. Blubber blocks out the cold, on shore or in the sea. ❸

## Stop and Think

❸ What does the lemming do to stay warm in the Arctic? How does the walrus stay warm?

The lemming _____

The walrus _____

# FOX IN WINTER

Foxes have a hard time spotting white rabbits and white lemmings. Their coats resemble the snow.

Yet, for the coldest part of the year, the Arctic fox is white, too. A white fox seems to vanish in the snow.

# FOX IN SUMMER

For a short part of the year, the Arctic fox is gray. A gray coat mimics the look of melting snow. It's hard to see this fox then, too. It blends right in. In fact, the Arctic fox is hard to spot any time of year! **4**

**Stop and Think**

**4** How can blending in help a hunting animal like the Arctic fox?

*Blending in can help a hunting animal by* _____

_____

_____

# POLAR BEAR

White coats can help Arctic animals sneak up on their next meal! The land here is quite flat. Animals can't hide behind a tree and wait for a meal to walk by. They hide another way. White predators are not obvious in white snow. These animals' white coats help them stay alive!

In fact, seeing nothing but white in the Arctic can be deceptive. A big white animal blends in well. It stays very still to lure small animals out of their dens. If a rabbit hears a snort, it may be too late to escape! **5**

## Stop and Think

**5** Why can't Arctic animals hide behind a tree?

*They can't hide behind a tree because* _____

_____

_____

# MUSK OX

The huge musk ox is not hard to spot. It does not need to hide. This animal has sharp horns that send other animals running.

An ox has two coats to keep out the cold. A top coat is long and thick. It hangs down to the ox's feet. An inside coat is soft, sort of like a sheep's. Think of how you would feel if you wore two coats! When the snow melts, the musk ox sheds the inside coat. It does not need it anymore. Still, it keeps its horns! **6**

## Stop and Think

**6** What two traits help the musk ox live in the Arctic?

*Two traits that help the musk ox live in the Arctic are*

_____

_____

# SNOW GEESE

Ducks and geese soar in the far north. Some come north in the spring and stay until fall. Some stay all year, often near the shore. They catch fish from seas or lakes. All have soft down to help protect them from the cold.

Were you born for snow? The Arctic has lots of snow. If you go, take your white coat. Then the foxes won't be able to spot you! **7**

## Stop and Think

**7** What are other animals that use color or patterns to survive?

*Other animals that use color or patterns to survive are*

_____

_____

# Think Critically

**1.** How does the weather in the Arctic affect the animals? Copy the chart, and fill it in. **CAUSE AND EFFECT**

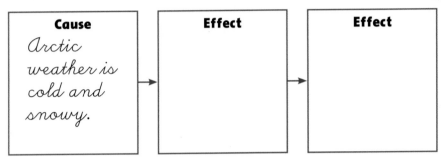

| Cause | Effect | Effect |
|-------|--------|--------|
| Arctic weather is cold and snowy. | | |

**2.** A main idea of the selection is that animals have ways to stay alive when food is scarce. What details support this? **MAIN IDEA AND DETAILS**

These are some supporting details: _____

_____

_____

**3.** Why did the author describe many kinds of Arctic animals? **AUTHOR'S PURPOSE**

The author described many kinds of Arctic animals

because _____

_____

_____

constant

contract

depths

eruption

gradually

immediate

revealed

# Vocabulary

## Build Robust Vocabulary

Read the selection and think about the meanings of the words in dark type.

Earth's crust is made up of big plates that shift around very **gradually.** This movement is often so slow that we can't feel it. Heat from the **depths** of the earth makes these plates bump into each other and crack. When the cracks grow bigger, melted rock escapes. This is called an **eruption.**

The plates press together all the time. This **constant** pressing makes the plates **contract.** If the plates slip or crack all of a sudden, the **immediate** result is an earthquake. Special instruments can record earthquake waves. Earthquake waves are like ripples in a pond. Records have **revealed** the path and strength of many past earthquakes.

What happens to the land when the earth moves? Can we escape earthquakes? You will find out when you read "When the Earth Moves."

**Write the Vocabulary Word that completes each sentence. The first one has been done for you.**

1. Plates bump into each other and crack. This happens because of the heat from the _____depths_____ of the earth.

2. When plates press together, they _____, or shrink.

3. Plates shift around very _____ . The movements are often very slow.

4. Records have _____ the strength of past earthquakes. These records tell us a lot about earthquakes.

5. When melted rock escapes from cracks in the earth, it is called an _____ .

6. If plates make a sudden movement, the _____ result is an earthquake.

7. Plates press together all the time. This _____ pressing makes them shrink.

magma

plate

plate

# When the Earth Moves

by Linda Barr • illustrated by Gary LaCoste

Have you ever felt the earth move? Why do earthquakes happen? How can you stay safe during and after an earthquake? Why does the earth move at all?

Let's start by looking at Earth's crust. This crust is 50 miles thick in some places, but thinner in others. It is made of layers of rock and dirt. The crust has cracks in it. Over time, these cracks have broken the crust into seven big plates and many smaller ones. **1**

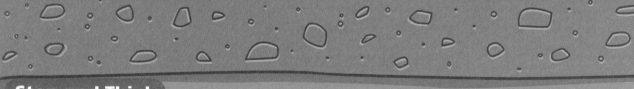

## Stop and Think

**1** What is Earth's crust made of?

Earth's crust is made of _____

_____

_____

The plates shift around. Much of the time they shift so gradually that you don't feel them move. It can take a year for the plates to travel just an inch.

Heat from the depths of Earth makes these big rock plates rub and bump into each other. This makes more cracks form. The cracks grow bigger and melted rock, or magma, can escape. This is called an eruption. These eruptions over time can make new mountains. **2**

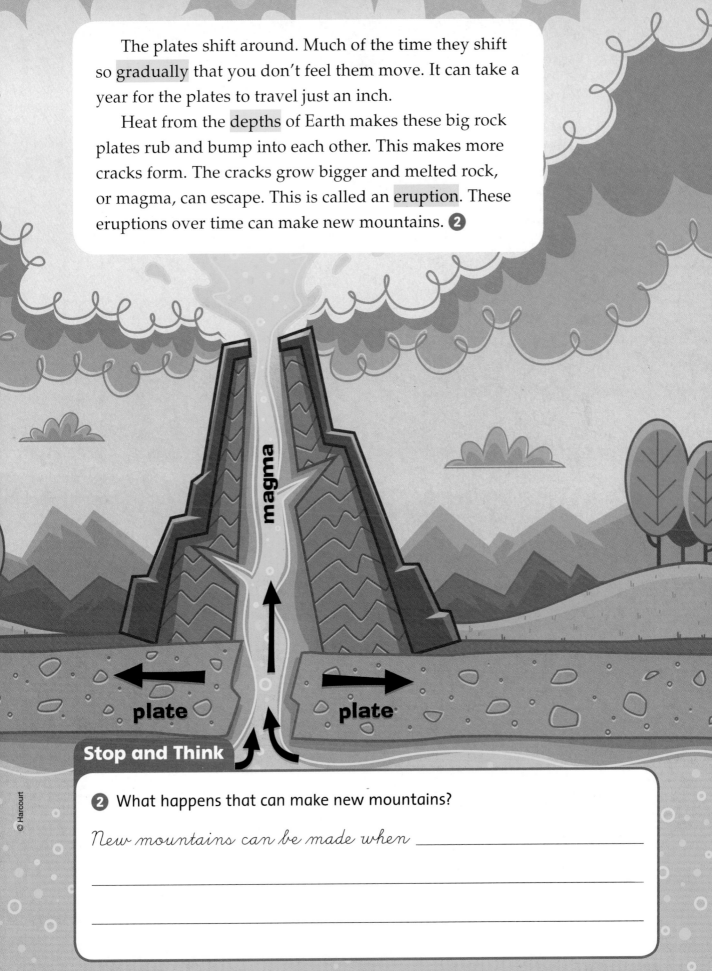

magma

plate        plate

**Stop and Think**

**2** What happens that can make new mountains?

*New mountains can be made when* _____

_____

_____

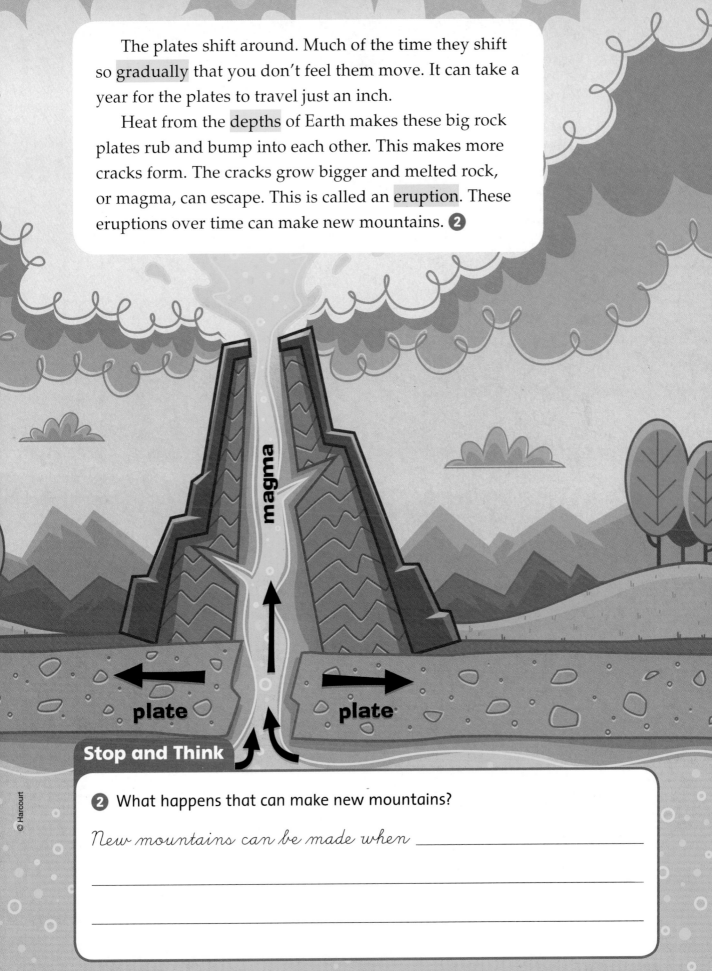

The plates press together in places. This constant pressing can make the plates shrink a bit. As they contract in this way, the plates can twist and bend. One plate may slip under another plate. Perhaps one of the plates cracks. Big blocks of rock may rise or fall.

This shifting makes many of the landforms we see. Blocks of rock can rise up to form mountains. Blocks can slip downward to make valleys. **3**

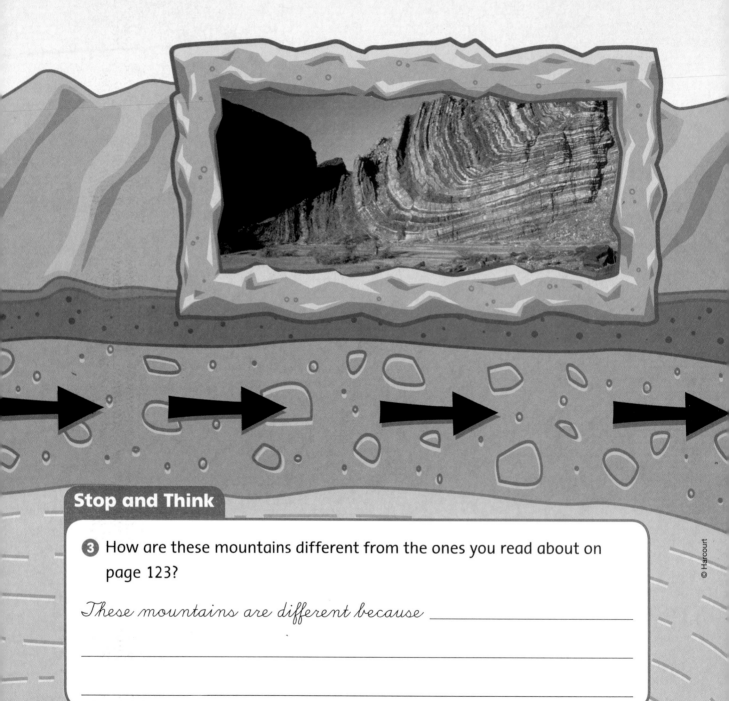

## Stop and Think

**3** How are these mountains different from the ones you read about on page 123?

*These mountains are different because* _____

_____

_____

Something else can happen, too. The plates may slip or crack all of a sudden. The immediate result of this sudden movement is an earthquake.

All earthquakes send out waves, like ripples on a pond. An earthquake can be so small that it can't be felt. A stronger earthquake sends out bigger waves and can be felt for hundreds of miles. Strong earthquakes can harm people and animals. They can bring down trees, crack roads, and destroy homes. ❹

Hey! Look out!

Oops. Sorry!

## Stop and Think

❹ How does an earthquake happen?

An earthquake happens when _____

_____

_____

A special instrument keeps records of earthquake waves and helps us learn. Records have revealed the path and strength of many past earthquakes.

We can use these records to predict where an earthquake may happen. Many occur where Earth's plates come together. You may have heard of earthquakes shaking up the West Coast. Two big plates press together along this coast. **5**

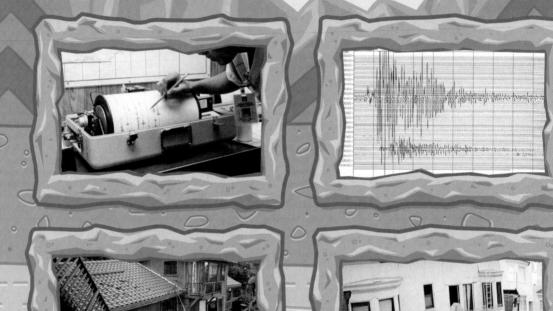

## Stop and Think

**5** How do you think people can stay safe during an earthquake?

*I think people can stay safe during an earthquake if they*

_____

_____

Once an earthquake starts, it may be too late to escape it. But there are steps you can take to stay safe. Inside, remember to drop, cover, and hold. First, drop to the floor. Second, cover yourself with your arms or duck under strong furniture. Third, hold on to something strong. Stay away from windows or things that could fall. Stay calm and help others do the same. Outside, get away from buildings, electrical lines, and other things that can fall. **6**

WOW!

It's okay!

MILK

**Stop and Think**

**6** Why should you cover yourself during an earthquake?

*I should cover myself during an earthquake because*

© Harcourt

After an earthquake, have an adult turn off the gas and water. Pipes crack and let out harmful gases. Broken pipes can also make water unsafe to drink.

Be prepared for what happens after a big earthquake or any natural disaster. Put together a kit of things you may need. This kit needs to include water, food, and a first-aid kit.

Earth's plates are moving all the time. Now you will understand why it is moving under your feet! ➐

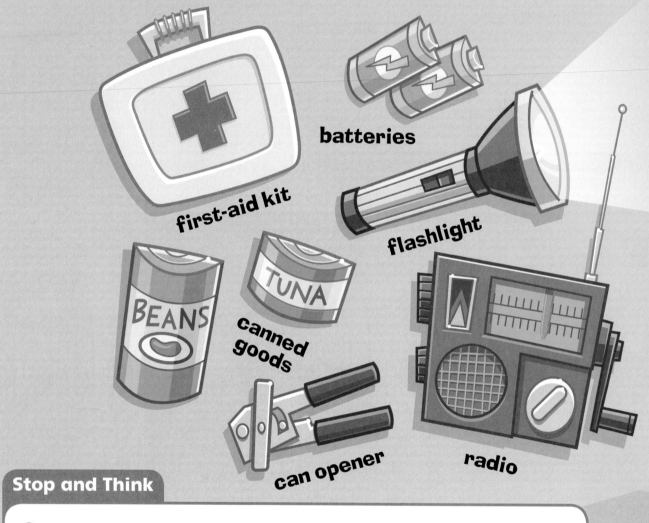

**batteries**

**first-aid kit**

**flashlight**

**BEANS**

**TUNA**

**canned goods**

**can opener**

**radio**

## Stop and Think

➐ What else do you think should be in an emergency kit?

*I think an emergency kit should also have* _____

_____

_____

# Think Critically

**1.** How does learning about past earthquakes help us today?
**DRAW CONCLUSIONS**

*Learning about past earthquakes can* _____

_____

_____

**2.** A strong earthquake happens. What are the effects of it? Copy the chart, and fill it in. **CAUSE AND EFFECT**

| Cause | Effect |
|-------|--------|
| *A strong earthquake sends out big waves.* → | |

**3.** Why does the author tell you about Earth's movements?
**AUTHOR'S PURPOSE**

*The author tells me about Earth's movements so*

_____

_____

altered

discouraged

drudgery

plunge

scoffed

skeptically

smoldering

treacherous

# Vocabulary

## Build Robust Vocabulary

Write the Vocabulary Word that completes each sentence. The first one has been done for you.

Jason's mom flew their plane a lot. When the wheels didn't go down, she gazed at the controls **(1)** _____skeptically_____ . Landing without wheels can be **(2)** _____ . The pilot has to land on the belly of the plane.

Jason thought he could smell smoke. Something seemed to be **(3)** _____ . His mom **(4)** _____ at his worry. She told him there was no fire and they would be home in a flash.

Jason's mom tested the wheels again.
Nothing. Jason could tell that his mom was getting

**(5)** _____ . Jason started to

shake. He was nervous. He was worried that they

were going to **(6)** _____ from

the sky and crash.

Jason always complained about his chores

at home. Now he wished he was back to that

**(7)** _____ . The airport controller

came on the radio. He wanted Jason's mom to slow

her speed. She **(8)** _____ the

plane's speed to help use up gas.

**Write the answers to these questions. Use complete
sentences.**

  **9.** Why do you think landing a plane without wheels
  is treacherous?

  _____

  _____

 **10.** Why do you think Jason thinks chores are **drudgery**?

  _____

  _____

# MOM in CONTROL

**by Sam Nori • illustrated by Steve Johnson & Lou Fancher**

Jason stared out the window of the small plane. The sky seemed hazy, but he didn't worry. His mom was the pilot. She had flown this two-seater many miles.

"We're getting close to the airport now," she told him. "It's time to lower the landing gear."

Jason expected the thump of the wheels locking down. Yet all he could hear was grinding under their feet. Then, even that stopped. ❶

## Stop and Think

❶ What do you think is making the grinding noise?

*I think the grinding noise is made by* _____

_____

_____

His mom peered at the controls skeptically. "We'll be okay," she said. "The wheels will go down this time."

But all they could hear was grinding. There was no thump. The landing gear was stuck! The plane didn't have wheels! Landing could be treacherous. "What can we do?" Jason whispered.

"We'll be okay," his mom repeated. She was staring at the controls. Then a red signal began flashing.

## Stop and Think

**2** What is the problem in the story?

*The problem in the story is* _____

_____

_____

Then Jason sensed something burning. There were no flames, but could he smell smoke? Something seemed to be smoldering. "I smell smoke!" Jason yelled.

His mom smiled. "You worry too much, Jason," she scoffed. "There isn't any fire, believe me."

Mom attempted to lower the wheels a third time. Grind, grind, and then nothing. The wheels were still stuck. Jason could tell that his mom was getting discouraged. ❸

## Stop and Think

❸ Why is Jason's mom getting discouraged?

*Jason's mom is getting discouraged because* _____

_____

_____

Were they going to plunge from the sky and crash?

"This is 3308," his mom told the airport controller. "I have lost my wheels. We are six miles out and need help!"

How Jason longed for home! He always complained about his chores. Now he could not wait to get back to that drudgery.

Then the controller said, "Drop your speed, 3308. That will give us time to get the trucks out." 4

## Stop and Think

4 What does Jason's mom mean when she says "I have lost my wheels"?

Jason's mom means that _____

_____

_____

Trucks? The controller had to mean fire trucks. His mom pulled back on a control. That altered the plane's speed and made them fly slower.

"Can . . . can we land with no wheels?" Jason asked. He could see the fields far below.

"Yep!" she said. "Pilots do it all the time. They slide down the runway on the plane's belly." ⑤

## Stop and Think

⑤ **Why do you think fire trucks are at the airport?**

*I think fire trucks are at the airport because* _____

_____

_____

"Don't worry, Jason. Pilots plan for a problem like this. I know what to do." His mom didn't seem worried.

"Jason, I want to try the landing gear one more time. Maybe the wheels will drop this time."

Jason nodded and looked out the window. By then, he could see the airport below them. Two fire units were near the runway.

Grind, grind, grind, and then, clunk! The wheels were down! "Mom!" Jason cried. **6**

## Stop and Think

**6** Why do you think Jason's mom is so calm?

*I think Jason's mom is calm because* _____

_____

_____

"Yes, it will be okay." His mom then spoke to the controller. They were set for a landing.

As the plane approached the runway, Jason peeked out the window. Now he could see men in uniforms by the runway. Jason was glad they were there, just in case.

The next thing he knew, the plane's wheels touched down, and the plane slowed to a stop. What a relief! His mom was his hero. ❼

## Stop and Think

❼ **What message does the author want you to understand from this story?**

*The author wants me to understand* _____

_____

_____

# Think Critically

**1.** What do you think Jason will say the next time his mom asks him to go on a plane ride? **CHARACTER**

*I think Jason will say* _____

_____

_____

**2.** What happens in the story? Copy the chart, and fill it in.

**MAIN IDEA AND DETAILS**

| Plot Events |
|---|
| 1. *Jason and Mom go flying in a plane.* |
| 2. *Mom can't get the wheels down.* |
| 3. |
| 4. |

**3.** Is the title a good one for this story? Explain your answer.

**MAKE JUDGMENTS**

*I think the title for this story is* _____

_____

_____

dashed

drab

fascinated

hermits

occasionally

peculiar

timid

trembling

# Vocabulary

## Build Robust Vocabulary

Read the story and think about the meanings of the words in dark type.

Skaters **dashed** back and forth on the frozen pond. Kim talked to a husband and wife. She had not seen these two before, and they **fascinated** her. She wasn't **timid** about talking to them.

Kim was **trembling** from the cold. It was **peculiar** that these two wore scarves, but no coats. The wife's scarf had bright stripes, not like Kim's **drab** scarf.

The next day, Kim asked her grandfather about the husband and wife. "They might like to be alone, like **hermits**," Grandfather said. Kim could understand that. She **occasionally** liked to be alone, too.

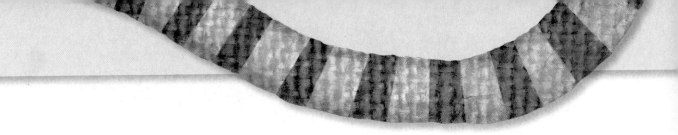

**Write the Vocabulary Word that completes each
sentence. The first one has been done for you.**

**1.** Kim likes to be alone _____occasionally_____ .
   But sometimes she likes to talk to someone.

**2.** Kim was shaking. She was _____
   from the cold.

**3.** The skaters _____ across the
   frozen pond.

**4.** The husband and wife were _____ .
   Something about them was not quite right.

**5.** They might be _____ who like to
   be alone.

**6.** The husband and wife were very interesting. They
   _____ Kim.

**7.** The wife's scarf had bright stripes. It was not

   _____ .

**8.** Kim isn't shy. She wasn't _____
   about talking to them.

# Just Down the Road

by Linda Barr • illustrated by Jamie Zollars

"My name is Kimheng," Kim told the husband and his wife, "but please call me Kim." Skaters dashed back and forth behind them. "My grandfather is right over there." Kim nodded at him.

"Yes," replied the wife with a bright smile. "We've met your grandfather, Mr. Hang."

"Is your home nearby?" Kim asked. She had not seen these two before, and they fascinated her.

"It is just down the road," the husband said. ❶

## Stop and Think

❶ Where does the story happen?

The story happens _____

_____

_____

142

By then, Kim was trembling from the cold. She tried to get closer to the fire. Yet these two stayed far from its heat and light.

"It's freezing," Kim said with a shiver. "It might even snow. Are you cold?" It was peculiar that the husband and his wife each wore a scarf but no coat.

"We're all right, thank you," replied the wife. Her scarf had bright stripes, not like Kim's drab one. Still, Kim's thick old scarf kept away the chill. **2**

## Stop and Think

**2** Why is it peculiar that the husband and wife are not wearing coats?

*It's peculiar that they are not wearing coats because* _____

_____

_____

Kim's grandfather walked over. "Someone made hot cocoa," he said.

"Yum!" Kim cried. "I'll get some right now! I want a pile of whipped cream on my cocoa!"

Her grandfather smiled and said to the husband and his wife, "Kim isn't timid when it comes to eating!"

The wife smiled and sighed. "We must skip the cocoa. I see it's getting late. It's time for us to go. But we're glad to have met you!" **3**

## Stop and Think

**3** What has Kim learned about the husband and wife so far?

*Kim has learned that they* _____

_____

_____

144

The husband and his wife walked out of sight.

"I'm glad I met you, too!" Kim yelled after them. All she could see now was the glow from their flashlight as it bobbed down the road.

Kim stared down the dark road. No homes were in sight. "They said their home was just down the road," she told her grandfather. "Maybe I can see it in daylight, but I can't see it now." ❹

## Stop and Think

❹ **What do you think Kim will do the next day?**

*I think Kim will* _____

_____

_____

Later the next day, Kim and her grandfather walked out to the road by the pond. Even in bright daylight, she could see no homes. Still, those two had no reason to lie.

"Their home might be far from the road, out of sight," Grandfather said. "They might like to be alone, like hermits."

Kim sighed and said, "You might be right. I occasionally like to be alone, too!" **5**

## Stop and Think

**5** Why do you think Kim cannot find the home of the husband and wife?

*I think Kim cannot find their home because* _____

_____

_____

©Harcourt

Still, Kim wondered, "Could we walk a little way? We might be able to see their home from there."

"All right," Grandfather replied. "Walking will be good for us. At least it's not as cold as it was last night."

They had walked for a while when Kim spotted something bright by the side of the road. She poked at it. "This looks like the scarf that the wife wore last night!" she cried. Then she spotted a flashlight under the pile of snow. **6**

## Stop and Think

**6** What does Kim spot by the side of the road?

Kim spots _____

_____

_____

"Oh, they must have died right here in the cold!" Kim cried. She looked up at her grandfather, who was smiling.

"They didn't die, Kim," he said. "They just melted when the sun came up."

Kim peered more closely at the piles of snow. She realized her grandfather was right. Then she started rolling a big snowball. "Do you think this is the right size for a snow girl?" she asked with a smile. **7**

## Stop and Think

**7** Why did the husband and wife melt?

*The husband and wife melted because* _____

_____

_____

148

# Think Critically

1. How would you describe Kim? **CHARACTER**

   *Kim is* _____

   _____

2. What is the problem in the story? How is it solved? Copy the chart, and fill it in. **PLOT**

   | Characters | Setting |
   | --- | --- |

   **Plot Events**

   1. Kim wants to know where the husband and wife are from.
   2.
   3.

3. There are clues in the story that the husband and wife were made of snow. What are these clues? **DRAW CONCLUSIONS**

   *These are the clues in the story:*

   _____

   _____

   _____

# Vocabulary

## Build Robust Vocabulary

Write the word that best completes each sentence.
The first one has been done for you.

1. Camping is a lot of fun for a beginner

   or a _____ **seasoned** _____ camper.

   **pristine   seasoned   deceptive**

2. Many adults still _____ the

   **cherish   hoist   lurk**

   times they went camping as kids.

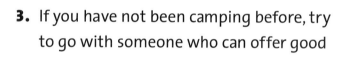

3. If you have not been camping before, try
   to go with someone who can offer good

   _____ .

   **drudgery   privilege   guidance**

4. Many campers think meals made outside taste

   _____ .

   **fragile   delectable   intrepid**

5. Even a hot dog will _____ taste

   **gradually   skeptically   undoubtedly**

   better when grilled over a roaring fire.

**6.** Many campers prefer a quiet, _____

**pristine    seasoned    intrepid**

forest for their campsite.

**7.** When it is very dry, the forest can be quite

_____ and at risk for fire.

**timid    discouraged    fragile**

**8.** Many campers have had the _____

**privilege    guidance    trait**

of camping in state parks.

**9.** _____ campers may want to see

**Delectable    Intrepid    Peculiar**

wild animals. It's best to stay away from them.

**10.** Let's _____ up our backpacks and

**cherish    plunge    hoist**

hit the trail!

**Write the answers to these questions. Use complete sentences.**

**11.** How does someone become a seasoned camper?

_____

_____

**12.** What is a pristine campsite like?

_____

_____

# The Camping Club

by Linda Barr

illustrated by Mike Tofanelli

## Characters

Narrator 1
Narrator 2
Kenneth Brown
Mrs. Brown
Kendra
David
Jenny
Chorus

**Narrator 1:** Summer is about over. But Mrs. Brown has a plan.

**David:** A camping club? Yes!

**Chorus:** That sounds like fun!

**David:** I have camped with my dad. He showed me how to set up camp.

**Chorus:** Sounds like David is a seasoned camper!

**Kendra:** Can girls go, too?

**Mrs. Brown:** Of course! I still cherish the times I camped as a girl.

**Kendra:** I know the right way to put out a fire.

**Mrs. Brown:** Good! We can use your guidance! ❶

## Stop and Think

❶ Why might Mrs. Brown know a lot about camping?

*Mrs. Brown might know a lot about camping because*

**David:** I learned first aid. I found out what to do if someone is drowning!

**Chorus:** Let's hope you won't need that!

**Kenneth:** What will we eat while we're camping, Mom?

**Mrs. Brown:** Something delectable and tasty. You all undoubtedly like hot dogs and beans, right?

**Jenny:** Maybe we could catch some trout in a stream!

**Mrs. Brown:** First, you all need to ask your parents if you can go. ②

**Stop and Think**

② What does Mrs. Brown need the kids to do first?

*First, Mrs. Brown needs the kids to* _____

_____

_____

**Narrator 2:** The next day, the kids rush back to the house.

**Kendra:** I can go, Mrs. Brown!

**David:** I just found out that I can go, too!

**Jenny:** Me, too! I can't wait!

**Mrs. Brown:** Good! I'll list some things you need to bring: food, bug spray, tents, sleeping bags. . . .

**Chorus:** That will be a lot of pounds to lift!

**Mrs. Brown:** Well, the campground is in a quiet, pristine forest. But it's also close to the road! ❸

**Stop and Think**

❸ Why does it matter if the camping supplies are heavy?

*It matters because* _____

_____

_____

© Harcourt

**Narrator 1:** On Friday, they arrive at the campground. They hoist up their backpacks and hike in.

**Narrator 2:** They set up the tents. They prowl around the forest. They eat hot dogs and beans. By sundown, the kids are tired.

**Chorus:** What is that buzzing sound?

**Kendra:** Pass the bug spray, please.

**Mrs. Brown:** Do you want to tell stories?

**Kenneth:** You'll have to shout a story to keep me awake! **4**

**Stop and Think**

**4** Imagine you want to buy some camping equipment. Where could you look to learn about what to buy?

I would look _____

_____

_____

© Harcourt

**Chorus:** What is that? It must be a big bug!

**Jenny:** Stop that!

**David:** It's not me! I'm not making a sound.

**Chorus:** There it is again!

**Mrs. Brown:** Now I hear it, too. But let's be intrepid campers. I'm sure it is nothing to be afraid of.

**Narrator 1:** Then something runs into camp.

**Chorus:** It's just a big dog!

**Mrs. Brown:** It must belong to a camper around here. ❺

**Stop and Think**

❺ Why does Jenny say "Stop that"?

*Jenny says "Stop that" because* _____

_____

_____

© Harcourt

156

**Narrator 1:** The dog barks and runs around.

**Kendra:** We won't get any sleep with this dog around!

**Chorus:** Time to find the owner!

**Narrator 2:** About an hour later, they find where the dog belongs. Back at camp, they all quickly fall asleep.

**Narrator 1:** The next morning, Kenneth wakes up first.

**Kenneth:** Time to get up!

**Mrs. Brown:** Not so loud! It's a privilege to camp here. We don't want to wake everyone up.

**Kenneth:** Sorry! How about a hike?

**David:** That sounds like a plan. **6**

## Stop and Think

**6** Why wouldn't the kids get any sleep with the dog around?

*The kids wouldn't get any sleep because* _____

_____

_____

**Narrator 1:** Hours later, it's time to go home.

**Mrs. Brown:** Let's put the fire out. The forest is fragile when it's dry. I'll put water on it and stir apart the ashes. Help me put dirt on the ashes and add more water.

**Kendra:** We have to make sure it's out all the way.

**Jenny:** We need this campground if we want to camp again.

**Mrs. Brown:** Right. In fact, would you kids like to make this trip again next year?

**Chorus:** That sounds like a good plan! **7**

## Stop and Think

**7** What do the campers do to put out the fire?

*To put out the fire, the campers* _____

_____

_____

158

© Harcourt

# Think Critically

**1.** Do you think the author wrote this play to tell you how to camp? Explain your answer. **AUTHOR'S PURPOSE**

*I think the author* _____

_____

_____

**2.** What event do you think the children will remember most from their camping trip? Explain your answer. **PLOT**

*The event I think the children will remember*

*most is* _____

_____

_____

**3.** Would you like to go camping? Explain.

**PERSONAL RESPONSE**

*I would* _____

_____

barriers

forged

hoaxer

perfect

quest

tinker

trampled

# Vocabulary

## Build Robust Vocabulary

Write the Vocabulary Word that completes each sentence in the selection. The first one has been done for you.

George Washington Carver was a farmhand on a

**(1)** _____quest_____ to fix a problem. After the

Civil War, he started to **(2)** _____ with

plants. He wanted to find different uses for them.

Carver was born a slave. After the Civil War, he

**(3)** _____ a life as a farmhand. The

land had been **(4)** _____ during the

war. It was hard to grow crops. Carver gave advice to

help farmers. He went on to invent many things made

from plants.

Inventors work to solve our problems. They want to invent things that make our lives better. Augustus Jackson was an inventor who set out to **(5)** _____ ice-cream flavors. Austin Kness was an inventor who made traps for mice. The traps had

**(6)** _____ to hold mice in place, but they did not hurt the mice. Frances Gabe invented a house that cleans itself. She was no **(7)** _____ .
It worked!

Inventors solve many problems. You will read more about them in "Inventors at Work."

# Inventors at Work

by Shannon Gilliam

illustrated by Alan Flinn

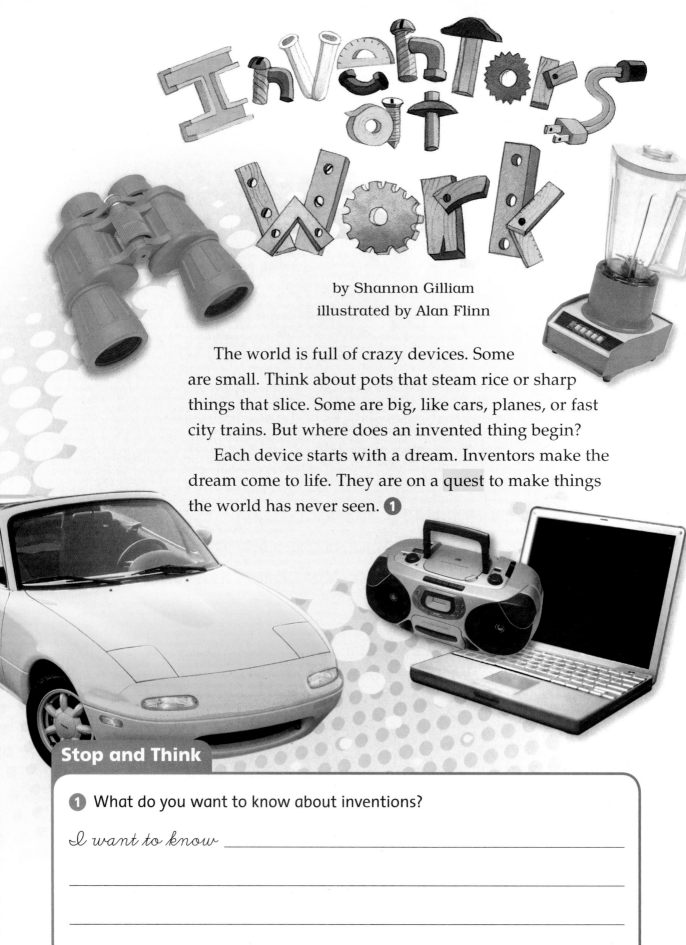

The world is full of crazy devices. Some are small. Think about pots that steam rice or sharp things that slice. Some are big, like cars, planes, or fast city trains. But where does an invented thing begin?

Each device starts with a dream. Inventors make the dream come to life. They are on a quest to make things the world has never seen. **1**

## Stop and Think

**1** What do you want to know about inventions?

*I want to know* _____

_____

_____

162

Frances Gabe had a dream. She made a house that cleans itself. It sounds like a joke. But Gabe is no hoaxer. Soap cleans her place at the press of a button. There is not a trace of dust when it dries!

Would you want a bed that you didn't have to make? Sarah Goode came up with a bed like that. It folds up after you sleep and saves a lot of space. It's excellent for small places. ❷

## Stop and Think

❷ What is the author's opinion about Sarah Goode's invention?

The author tells us _____

_____

_____

George Washington Carver faced many problems. He was born a slave, but was freed after the Civil War. After that, he was all alone. Carver forged a life as a farmhand.

Carver could see that the land around him was a mess. The Civil War had left its mark. Much of the land had been trampled. Some land had been burned. Farmers didn't know what to plant. Carver raced to fix the problem. He gave advice to help farmers. They called him the "Plant Doctor." ❸

## Stop and Think

❸ What do you think George Washington Carver will make from plants?

*Carver will use plants* _____

_____

_____

Carver began to tinker with plants. He came up with new ideas and kept notes. After much hard work, he would announce what he had found. Over the years, he introduced many new plants for farmers to grow.

Carver also invented hundreds of different uses for crops. He made candy, paper, and paste—all from plants. Do you know how he made a fancy face cream? With peanuts! ❹

## Stop and Think

❹ What did Carver do before he started inventing new things?

Carver spent his time _____

_____

_____

Augustus Jackson also worked with peanuts. However, he didn't make a face cream. He made ice cream. He had just one rule: Make choice ice cream for his city's citizens.

Jackson set out to perfect certain ice-cream flavors. His ice cream was such a big hit that he decided to sell it in huge tin cans. His ice cream sold in places all over the city. Augustus Jackson was the city's finest ice-cream producer. **5**

## Stop and Think

**5** How do you think Jackson felt about his new flavors for ice cream?

I think Jackson felt _____

_____

_____

Inventors work hard to fix problems. In 1897, mice were a problem for James Atkinson. There were too many! He made the world's first mouse trap. The device had a snap to hold mice in place. It wasn't fancy, but it was a fine trap. It wasn't so nice for mice, however.

Since the first trap sold well, there was no need to make a better device. No one paid it much mind. No one except Austin Kness. He got excited and decided to make the trap better. Kness came up with something that caught mice but did not hurt them. Barriers kept the mice in place. **6**

**Stop and Think**

**6** Which mouse trap would you buy? Explain your answer.

*I would buy* _____

_____

_____

Barbara Askins is an inventor, but she didn't make a device. She came up with an exciting process. She found a better way to process film. This new process made it possible to look at snapshots taken in space. We still use her process to look at x-rays and restore old snapshots.

What devices will the world need next? What processes can help us? It will take a top inventor to show the way. Maybe that certain inventor will be you! 7

## Stop and Think

7 Why does the author ask what devices the world needs next?

*The author asks what devices the world needs next because*

168

# Think Critically

1. What have you learned about inventions? Copy the chart, and fill it in. **MAIN IDEA AND DETAILS**

| K What I Know | W What I Want to Know | L What I Learned |
|---|---|---|
|  |  |  |

2. Why did Austin Kness make a new mouse trap? **CAUSE AND EFFECT**

   *Kness made a new mouse trap because* _____

   _____

   _____

3. Why do you think the author wrote the article? **AUTHOR'S PURPOSE**

   *The author wrote this article to* _____

   _____

   _____

ancestors

brilliant

exotic

graceful

mischievous

participate

# Vocabulary

## Build Robust Vocabulary

Write the Vocabulary Word that completes each sentence in the postcards. The first one has been done for you.

Dear Rex,

This postcard shows a fantastic painting by Diego Rivera. He liked to show the history of his Mexican **(1)** _____ancestors_____ . One time, Rivera played a good trick on someone. I'll tell you more about this **(2)** _____ artist when I get home.

Your pal,
Kate

Rex Davidson
4582 Main Street
Mansfield, Ohio 44902

Dear Brenda,

Faith Ringgold made the quilt shown on this postcard. It has such **(3)** _____ colors. See how bright they are! Ringgold's mom made art. Her mom urged her to **(4)** _____ and make art, too.

See you later,
Kate

Brenda Porter
13 Applewood Drive
Mansfield, Ohio 44902

Dear Tiffany,

This painting is by Georgia O'Keeffe. I think the flowers look strange and **(5)** _____ . It's like they came from a faraway land. But the lines in the painting are so soft and **(6)** _____ . I love to look at them!

Later,
Kate

Tiffany Martin
802 Fifth Street
Mansfield, Ohio 44902

# The Artist's Life

by Jimmy Aguilar

The life of an artist can start at any age. Georgia O'Keeffe showed a gift for art as a child. Her teachers told her to be an artist. They challenged her to fill pages with art.

Georgia O'Keeffe made art that was larger than life. She painted small flowers as giant ones. Her graceful lines made the giant flowers look exotic. She also painted the land around her. She hoped to show why she liked New Mexico's land so much. She felt large works would best show what she liked about the land.

At 96, Georgia O'Keeffe found new ways to do things. She began to make clay art. Even at an old age, she still made art. **1**

*Georgia O'Keeffe*

**Stop and Think**

**1** Why do you think Georgia O'Keeffe painted large works? Underline the words on the page that tell you.

*I think Georgia O'Keeffe painted large works because* _____

_____

_____

# Diego Rivera

Diego Rivera got an early start as well. He began studying art at age ten. His dad told him to leave Mexico to study in Spain. The artist was just a teenager.

Rivera later returned home. He made large paintings to show the history of his ancestors. He felt that the best art challenges the way we think.

In 1933, a man asked Rivera to paint an original work of art. The artist started a large painting. The man didn't like it. He told Rivera to change it, but Rivera would not budge. The painting was hidden and later smashed. But the mischievous artist got the last word. He had made a copy of his painting and displayed it anyway. ❷

## Stop and Think

❷ In Diego Rivera's opinion, what is the best art?

In Diego Rivera's opinion, the best art is _____

_____

_____

Faith Ringgold emerged as an artist at an early age, too. Her mom made art. She urged Ringgold to participate. Now Ringgold is all grown up. She has kids of her own.

Ringgold makes large quilts. Each quilt is made up of fun shapes and blocks. The shapes are brilliant shades, such as red and yellow. The edges of the quilts make a frame. Each frame leads to a strange and fantastic world.

Artists often show the same thing in more than one artwork. Ringgold shows bridges in many quilts. The bridge in this quilt is in New York City where Ringgold lives. **3**

*Faith Ringgold*

## Stop and Think

**3** How did Faith Ringgold's mom help her become an artist?

*Faith Ringgold's mom helped her become an artist when she*

**E**ach of these artists got an early start. They made original works as kids. They wanted their art to change the world.

Do you want an artist's life? It takes energy. It takes work. You can start with some paints or a wedge of clay. An artist's life can begin at any age. **4**

## Stop and Think

**4** How do you think the author feels about artists?

*I think the author* _____

_____

_____

© Harcourt

# Think Critically

**1.** How are Georgia O'Keeffe and Diego Rivera alike? How are they different? **COMPARE AND CONTRAST**

*Here's how they are alike:* _____

_____

_____

*Here's how they are different:* _____

_____

_____

**2.** Find an opinion about Faith Ringgold's art. Then copy the chart, and fill it in. **FACT AND OPINION**

| Fact | Opinion |
|------|---------|
| *Ringgold makes large quilts.* | |
| **Evidence** | **Evidence** |
| | *This statement cannot be proven. Some people might disagree.* |

**3.** How does an artist's life affect his or her artwork? **MAKE INFERENCES**

*An artist's life affects his or her artwork because* _____

_____

_____

**bountiful**

**inadvertently**

**intentions**

**relentless**

**resourceful**

**roused**

**stature**

**vast**

# Vocabulary

## Build Robust Vocabulary

Read the story and think about the meanings of the words in dark type.

Mr. and Mrs. Bright had five children. One liked to talk. Another was an artist. One was very **resourceful** and could come up with good plans. Another was calm and practical. And there was a quiet, clever one, too. The fields of their town were rich with dark soil and **bountiful** crops.

The land beyond the river was **vast.** Folks of gigantic **stature** lived there. These giants were very happy and noisy. Night after night, the **relentless** sound of their singing went on and on. Their twirling dances **inadvertently** stirred up a terrible wind.

Every night, the Brights were **roused** from their sleep by the loud noise and strong wind. The smartest of the children went to see the giants. He had good **intentions.** But can someone so little fix a giant problem?

**Write the Vocabulary Word that completes each sentence. The first one has been done for you.**

1. The fields were _____ bountiful _____ . They had a lot of crops.

2. Beyond the river was a _____ land with a lot of space.

3. The giants didn't mean to make so much noise. They _____ kept the Brights awake.

4. The giants' singing never stopped. It was

_____ .

5. The noise and wind woke up the Brights. It _____ them from their sleep.

6. One of the Bright kids was _____ . She could come up with plans to fix problems.

7. One of the children wanted to help. He had good

_____ .

8. The giants were of a tall _____ .

# Troy Bright
## Saves the Day

by Bill McMahon • illustrated by Steve Adams

In a land far away, there lived a family. Mr. and Mrs. Bright were the smartest grown-ups around. They had five smart and talented children.

Trevor, the oldest, was always first to speak. The second child, Tracey, was resourceful. She made plans in a snap. The third child, Tim, was an amazing artist. Tanya, the fourth, was calm and practical.

Little Troy was the smartest of them all. But nobody knew it because he was such a quiet boy. ❶

## Stop and Think

❶ How is Troy the same as the other Bright children? How is he different?

Troy is the same as the other Bright children because _____

_____

He is different because _____

The Bright family lived in a town called Littleton. Littleton's fields were rich with dark soil and bountiful crops. People enjoyed the town's many trees and flowers. There was even a calm river at the edge of town where people liked to fish and swim.

Littleton was a quiet little town, perfect in almost every way. But it was not free from all problems. At the time of our tale, Littleton was facing two big problems. *Giant* problems, you might say. **2**

## Stop and Think

**2** For a town like Littleton, what might be a giant problem?

*For a town like Littleton, a giant problem might be* _____

_____

_____

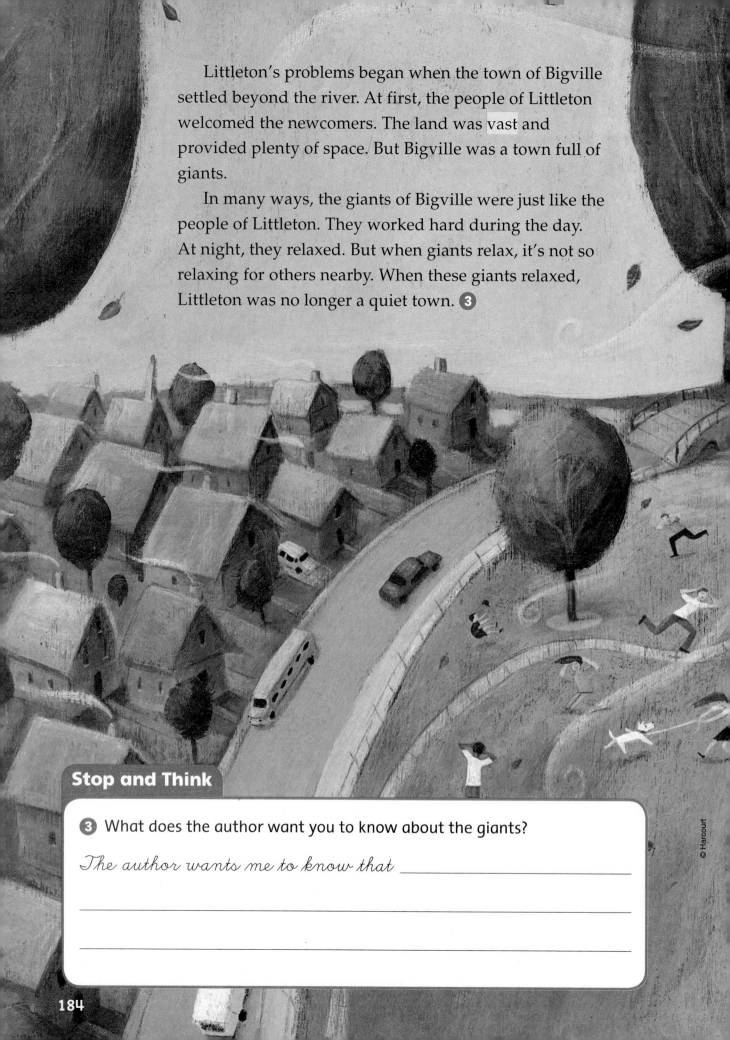

Littleton's problems began when the town of Bigville settled beyond the river. At first, the people of Littleton welcomed the newcomers. The land was vast and provided plenty of space. But Bigville was a town full of giants.

In many ways, the giants of Bigville were just like the people of Littleton. They worked hard during the day. At night, they relaxed. But when giants relax, it's not so relaxing for others nearby. When these giants relaxed, Littleton was no longer a quiet town. **3**

## Stop and Think

**3** What does the author want you to know about the giants?

The author wants me to know that _____

_____

_____

The giants met to sing their favorite tunes. But every time they sang, the people of Littleton had to run for their homes! The giants' voices were so loud that the folks of Littleton had to hide inside to escape. Every night, the relentless noise hurt their ears!

Besides singing, the giants loved to dance. They joined hands and spun around. But all this whirling and twirling inadvertently stirred up a terrible wind. It rattled the walls and windows. It ripped the leaves off the trees. ❹

## Stop and Think

❹ How do the giants cause problems for Littleton?

*The giants cause problems for Littleton when they* _____

_____

_____

© Harcourt

Every night the people of Littleton were roused from their sleep. Something had to be done. The Bright family called a town meeting to discuss the problems.

Trevor was first to speak. He suggested they put cotton in their ears to block out the noise. But Tracey pointed out that this would not stop the wind. She wanted to put up a wall. Tim agreed and offered to paint it. Then, practical Tanya said that a wall wouldn't be high enough. At best, it would only reach the giants' ankles. **5**

## Stop and Think

**5** How would you solve Littleton's problems?

*I would solve Littleton's problems by* _____

_____

_____

© Harcourt

Everyone groaned. Even the Brights couldn't solve the problem. But Troy was thinking. He felt big problems called for big ideas.

The next morning Troy visited the giants. They had no idea that their singing was hurting people's ears. They were also shocked to learn that they could create such a wind. They promised to never sing or dance again. Troy saw that the giants had good intentions, but he could not ask them to stop having fun. Besides, now he had a big idea. **6**

## Stop and Think

**6** What do you think Troy's big idea will be?

*I think Troy's big idea will be* _____

_____

_____

Troy saw the giant stature of everything in Bigville. Grass was as tall as Troy's chest. Huge trees seemed to reach up to the clouds. Troy asked the giants to plant more of these trees along the river.

A forest was planted in no time. It was just the thing to block a noisy song or a terrible wind. Now the giants could sing and dance without hurting the people of Littleton.

Now, sometimes at night, music drifts over the trees and across the river. When it does, the people of Littleton dance right along. **7**

**Stop and Think**

**7** What message does the author want you to understand from this story?

*The author wants me to understand that* _____

_____

_____

188

# Think Critically

1. What are the main events in this story? Copy the chart, and fill it in. **PLOT**

| **Plot Events** |
| --- |
| 1. |
| 2. |
| 3. |
| 4. |

2. Why do the giants plant a forest? **CAUSE AND EFFECT**

*The giants plant a forest because* _____

_____

_____

_____

3. How would you describe Troy? **CHARACTER'S TRAITS**

*Troy is* _____

_____

_____

anxiously

confidently

declared

distressed

gloated

insisted

magnificent

# Vocabulary

## Build Robust Vocabulary

Write the Vocabulary Word that completes each sentence in the story. The first one has been done for you.

## An Awful Mess

Five exhausted workers were walking home. "It is so awfully hot and humid," each **(1)** _____declared_____ . They needed a place to rest. Then they spotted a nice bit of lawn. It was a **(2)** _____ place to have a nap.

"I saw it first! Ha! This nice space is all mine," one worker **(3)** _____ .

"No, I saw it first! It's mine!" each worker

**(4)** _____ .

They all rested on the grass. One by one, they fell asleep on the lawn.

© Harcourt

When they woke up, they saw that they were in
an awful mess. They had slept until dawn, and their
ten feet were all mixed up! They bawled and yelled until
a child came by. "My name is Paula. You all seem awfully

**(5)** _____ . What's the matter?"

she asked.

"We're all mixed up!" the workers cried

**(6)** _____ .

"Don't worry, I can fix this problem," Paula said

**(7)** _____ .

How will Paula fix this awful mess?

# An Awful Mess

retold by Jimmy Aguilar

illustrated by Kevin Rechin

It was just about the end of a hot August day. Five workers set down their five saws and started for home.

"It is so awfully hot and humid," said one.

"Yes, so awfully hot and humid," each declared.

Then they spotted a nice bit of lawn. "I saw it first! Ha! This nice space is all mine," gloated one worker.

"No, I saw it first! It is mine!" each insisted.

They all rested side by side on the grass.

One by one, they fell asleep. ❶

## Stop and Think

❶ How do you know the workers take a nap?

*I know this because* _____

_____

_____

192

It was dawn when the first worker woke up. "How awful!" he said. "We slept until dawn!"

"Awful, indeed!" each repeated as they woke up.

"We'll be late for work if we go home now."

"But we must go home."

"Wait! We can't go anyplace," bawled one. "Look. Our feet are all mixed up!" They saw that he was right. There were ten scrawny feet. But their feet were in such a tangle, they could not tell to whom each belonged. **2**

## Stop and Think

**2** Why are the workers upset?

*The workers are upset because* _____

_____

_____

"What an awful mess!" they bawled. "We'll be on this lawn for the remainder of our days."

"It's all your fault," said one worker to the next.

"No, it's your fault! It's your fault!" each repeated.

Just then a child happened by. "Hello," she said. "My name is Paula. You all seem awfully distressed. What's the matter?"

"We're in an awful mess," they bawled. "We're stuck."

"Stuck?" asked Paula. "How can that be?" ③

## Stop and Think

③ How do the workers act when they discover they have a problem?

*When the workers discover they have a problem, they*

_____

_____

"Because we can't tell whose feet belong to whom!"

Paula was in awe. Could these five workers be kidding? She would kid them, too.

"You can't stay on this lawn," Paula teased. "It's against the law. If you are caught here, you could get a big fine. You might even be hauled away."

"Oh, no!" a worker said anxiously. "If we were caught by the law, that could be awful for us!"

"Very awful, indeed!" each repeated. "What can we do?" **4**

## Stop and Think

**4** What do you think will happen next?

*I think* _____

_____

_____

"They can't haul us away!" one cried. "We're stuck on this lawn."

"Maybe they'll bring a big truck," Paula said.

"Oh, oh! What an awful mess," the first worker cried.

"Yes! An awful, awful mess," each worker bawled.

Now Paula saw how upset the workers really were. They weren't kidding at all. She began to wish she had not teased them so much. **5**

Ouch!

## Stop and Think

**5** How do you think these workers usually act when they have a problem?

*I think the workers usually* _____

_____

_____

"Don't worry anymore. I can fix this problem," Paula said confidently. "Just watch." She picked up a small twig. Then she gave a light poke to one of the ten scrawny feet sprawled on the lawn.

"Ouch," said one worker. "Something poked me."

"That must be your foot," said Paula. "Draw it in, please."

Paula gave another light poke.

"Ouch," said another worker. "Something poked me!"

"That must be one of yours," Paula repeated. "Draw it in, please."

Paula poked each of the feet until the very last worker was standing up. **6**

## Stop and Think

**6** How would you describe Paula?

*Paula is* _____

_____

_____

All five workers were overcome with joy. "You fixed this awful mess," each declared. "Now they can't haul us away."

"There is no need to haul you away. But I hope all this has taught you a lesson," said Paula.

"It's taught us a big lesson," they said.

"Yes. It's taught us a magnificent lesson."

"What lesson has it taught you?" asked Paula.

The workers smiled. "Never, ever fall asleep on a lawn!"

## Stop and Think

**7** How does the author make you laugh with this story?

*The author makes me laugh when he* _____

_____

_____

# Think Critically

**1.** How does Paula help the rabbits? **PLOT**

*Paula helps the rabbits when she* _____

_____

_____

**2.** How would you describe the rabbits? **CHARACTER'S TRAITS**

*The rabbits are* _____

_____

_____

**3.** What message does the author want you to learn from this story? Copy the chart, and fill it in. **THEME**

| Characters' Actions | Characters' Motivations | Setting |
|---|---|---|
| *The rabbits cry and fight.* | *They want to get up.* | *on a lawn* |

**Theme**

# Vocabulary

## Build Robust Vocabulary

Write the word that best completes each sentence.
The first one has been done for you.

1. One day, when two pals are at the beach, a crime is
   _____ **exposed** _____ !

   **installed   insisted   exposed**

2. It starts when Danny's mom is _____

   **gracious   ominous   trampled**

   and packs a lunch for the boys.

3. Danny _____ with pride when

   **beams   participates   tinkers**

   Owen says his mom's peanut butter cookies are
   the best.

4. "Let's eat! I know where I left our lunch basket," Owen

   says with _____ .

   **stature   barriers   self-assurance**

5. "What _____ luck!" yells Owen. Their

   **gracious   miserable   bountiful**

   picnic basket is missing!

**6.** "Someone took it. We should have

_____ an alarm!"

**declared   distressed   installed**

**7.** The boys feel that a day without lunch is

_____ before them.

**looming   graceful   forged**

**8.** "Why didn't we _____ our picnic

**participate   monitor   confound**

basket better?" the boys ask.

**9.** Then two officers come up to them and say, "Did

something _____ you? You look

**confound   monitor   perfect**

confused about something."

**10.** Then the boys and the officers hear a loud,

_____ sound. What could it be?

**vast   ominous   gracious**

**Write the answers to these questions. Use complete
sentences.**

**11.** How does a gracious person treat others?

_____

_____

**12.** If a sound is ominous, how does it make you feel?

_____

_____

# The Case of the Seashore Crook

by Shannon Gilliam • illustrated by Laura Freeman-Hines

## CAST OF CHARACTERS

| | |
|---|---|
| Narrator 1 | Owen |
| Narrator 2 | First Officer |
| Narrator 3 | Second Officer |
| Narrator 4 | Shannon |
| Danny | Chorus |

**Narrator 1:** Danny and Owen stood on the beach as the tide lapped at their feet. Their bellies growled with hunger. They couldn't wait to eat.

**Owen:** I'm starving!

**Danny:** My mom packed us a lunch basket. I left it just down the beach so it would be close when it was time to eat. ❶

## Stop and Think

❶ Where are Danny and Owen?

*Danny and Owen are* _____

_____

_____

**Danny:** She packed two sandwiches, water, a bunch of grapes, and plenty of peanut butter cookies.

**Owen:** All right! Your mom's cookies are the best. I could eat two baskets of those cookies.

**Narrator 2:** As he scanned the beach, Owen's self-assurance vanished. He wouldn't be eating any cookies right away.

**Narrator 3:** Because when they arrived at the spot where the basket should be, a terrible crime was exposed.

**Chorus:** Or so it seemed to them at the time. . . . ❷

## Stop and Think

❷ How does Owen feel about the cookies?

*Owen feels that the cookies* _____

_____

_____

**Danny:** Owen, the picnic basket is missing! And that means all of our goodies are missing, too!

**Owen:** Wow! What miserable luck! How could this have happened?

**Danny:** I'll tell you how. Some crook must have taken it.

**Owen:** What kind of crook would take a picnic basket?

**Danny:** The hungry kind, I suppose.

**Narrator 4:** The boys looked up and down along the beach, but they didn't see any trace of a crook. ③

**Stop and Think**

③ Why do Danny and Owen look up and down the beach?

*Danny and Owen look up and down the beach because* _____

_____

_____

**Narrator 1:** Danny and Owen were lucky. Two police officers were close by.

**First Officer:** You two look like you need help. What seems to be the problem here?

**Owen:** A crook took his picnic basket.

**Danny:** I should have kept a better lookout.

**Owen:** We should have installed an alarm!

**Second Officer:** Well, let's not assume foul play.

**First Officer:** Maybe it wasn't a crook who took it. ④

## Stop and Think

**④ What do the officers tell Danny and Owen?**

*The officers tell Danny and Owen* _____

_____

_____

**Second Officer:** Why would a crook want your basket?

**Owen:** His mom's cookies were in there!

**Narrator 2:** Danny beams with pride over this compliment.

**First Officer:** Your mom was very gracious to make such a tasty lunch, but a crook would not know she's such a good cook.

**Second Officer:** We monitor this beach every day. We saw no one prowling around. And look, no footprints.

**Chorus:** Wow, no footprints! That's strange!

**First Officer:** It does confound things a bit. It seems we have a mystery looming before us.

**Owen:** But what happened to our basket? ❺

## Stop and Think

❺ **What do you think happened to the basket?**

*I think the basket was* _____

_____

_____

**Narrator 3:** Suddenly, they heard an ominous sound not far away.

**Narrator 4:** A mighty wave crashed to shore. They all peered out to sea.

**Danny:** Look, I see the basket! It's in the water!

**Second Officer:** Hmmm, perhaps the high tide had something to do with it.

**Owen:** Good thing it's a wooden basket. It's still floating.

**Danny:** Now what should we do?

**First Officer:** The waves might bring it back to shore. **6**

## Stop and Think

**6** What was the ominous sound they heard?

*The ominous sound was* _____

_____

_____

**Second Officer:** You could just wait for someone to bring it back.

**Narrator 1:** The officer points to a person in a kayak.

**Owen:** Hey! Someone *is* getting our basket!

**Danny:** That's my sister. Shannon! Can you help?

**Narrator 2:** Shannon pulls the basket from the water.

**Narrator 3:** She waves. Then she pulls out the cookies.

**Danny:** Okay, Shannon! We'll share. Just save some for us!

**First Officer:** Shouldn't be a long wait now. The waves are bringing her in.

**Owen:** I just hope she leaves us some cookies! **7**

## Stop and Think

**7** What lesson do the boys learn?

*The boys learn that* _____

_____

_____

# Think Critically

**1.** How does the picnic basket end up in the water? **CAUSE AND EFFECT**

*The picnic basket ends up in the water because*

_____

_____

**2.** Why are there no footprints on the beach? **DRAW CONCLUSIONS**

*There are no footprints because* _____

_____

_____

**3.** What was the mystery? How was it solved? **PLOT**

*The mystery was* _____

_____

_____

consisted

intends

prideful

recalls

select

snatched

# Vocabulary

## Build Robust Vocabulary

Read the story and think about the meanings of the words in dark type.

Sue is always the new girl in town. Her dad's work has always **consisted** of traveling. Sue knows her dad wants her to be happy. He often **recalls** what it was like to be her age. He wants her to be happy, but Sue still gets lonely.

Not long ago, Sue found a dog at her new home. She **snatched** some ham and rushed out to feed him. Sue made a new friend. She feels **prideful** about this now. Making a new friend is not always easy.

Sue isn't sure if her dad will like the dog. He only likes a few **select** dogs. Sue **intends** to ask him if the dog can stay.

**Write the Vocabulary Word that completes each sentence. The first one has been done for you.**

**1.** Sue's dad _____ **recalls** _____ what it was like to be her age.

**2.** Sue's life with her dad has _____ of a lot of traveling.

**3.** Sue's dad might not let her keep the dog. She _____ to ask him.

**4.** Her dad doesn't like all dogs, but he does like a few _____ dogs.

**5.** Sue _____ some ham and ran to feed the dog.

**6.** Sue feels _____ because she made a friend.

**Write the Vocabulary Word that best completes the synonym web.**

**7.**

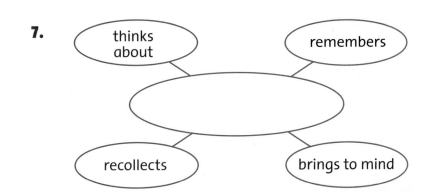

# My New Dog

by Guadalupe V. Lopez
illustrated by Jim Madsen

My name is Sue. I am the new girl. I'm always the new girl. You see, Dad's work has always consisted of traveling. I've seen most of the country. It sounds like fun, right? But it's not. It sometimes gets lonely. I wish I could unpack my suitcase for good.

I start fifth grade soon. I worry and wonder. Are the kids in this new town nice? I hope so. I'm not so good at chitchat, so I'm quiet. I only talk when I have something to say. ❶

## Stop and Think

❶ How does Sue feel about moving so much?

*Sue feels that moving* _____

_____

_____

A while back, I decided to start a journal. Now I write and scribble in it all day. It contains a life story. But not about a girl named Sue. It is about Lucinda, a girl I sometimes pretend to be.

"Sue, go outside. Don't stay cooped up in here," ordered Dad one day. "It's past noon. It's a fantastic day. Go on."

I realize Dad wants the best for me. He often recalls what it was like to be my age, and he wants me to be happy. He wants me to have lots of friends. ❷

## Stop and Think

❷ What do you think it means when Dad says "Don't stay cooped up in here"?

*I think Dad means that* _____

_____

© Harcourt

Outside, I opened my journal to start a new chapter: *Lucinda rested on the stoop. A cool breeze swirled her golden curls. She peered down the grimy avenue.*

I peered down my own grimy road. At first I didn't see the dog limping up the road. He limped right up to my porch.

"What's the matter, pooch?" I examined his leg. No wonder. A big thorn was stuck in his paw. Tenderly, I pulled it loose. He gazed up at me. Then he grinned a goofy grin. I had never seen a dog do that before! **3**

### Stop and Think

**3** Why is the dog limping?

*The dog is limping because* _____

_____

_____

The dog's fur was brown and nappy, like an old, droopy teddy bear. He could use some grooming to get his fur smooth again.

I examined him for a tag. But there was nothing, not even a collar.

"Well, you need a name. How about Teddy?" I asked. He barked and seemed to approve.

"Next, you need food. Wait here," I said. Teddy plopped down next to the stoop. **4**

## Stop and Think

**4** Why does Sue name the dog Teddy?

Sue names the dog Teddy because _____

_____

_____

I went into the kitchen. I snatched some ham off a plate and rushed back outside. Teddy was happy to see me. He was just plain gleeful to see the ham. Snatching it up, he didn't even chew it.

Teddy came visiting every day after that. He'd stay a bit. Then he'd go off to explore. I don't know where he went. He just moved on. I realized that he was just like me. He didn't stay in one place too long. But when he was at my place, we had fun. **5**

## Stop and Think

**5** Where does the story take place? What has happened in the story so far?

The story takes place _____

So far, _____

_____

We played a sport I call broom ball, a game I created for Teddy. I'd use the broom to shoot a rubber ball through a hoop. Teddy would scoop the ball up in his mouth. Then he would drop it at my feet, and I'd shoot again. That ball was covered with dirty drool. Good thing I had the broom! Sometimes Dad would come out and be our audience.

My time with Teddy made me want to have a home. I didn't want him to go away each day. I wanted Teddy to stay. I knew I had to talk to Dad. **6**

## Stop and Think

**6** Do you think Dad will let Teddy stay? Explain your answer.

*I think Dad will* _____

_____

_____

"Daddy, do you like dogs?" I asked.

"Well, I don't like *all* dogs. I like a few select dogs. I *do* like Teddy," he said.

"Do you like it here, Dad?" I asked. I shifted back and forth on my feet.

"I intend to work here. Should we stay here?" he asked. "Should Teddy stay, too?"

I nodded and gave Dad a big hug.

"Come on, boy," exclaimed Dad, looking prideful about our home. He waved Teddy toward our front door. "Welcome home." **7**

## Stop and Think

**7** Why do you think Sue asks Dad if he likes dogs?

*I think Sue asks Dad if he likes dogs because* _____

_____

_____

# Think Critically

**1.** How does the story end? Copy the chart, and fill it in. **CHARACTER, SETTING, PLOT**

| Characters | Setting |
|---|---|

**Plot Events**
1. *Sue meets Teddy.*
2. *Teddy comes to visit all the time.*
3.

**2.** How do you think the author feels about moving a lot? Why do you think so? **AUTHOR'S PURPOSE**

*I think the author feels* _____

_____

_____

**3.** At first, Dad does not let Teddy into the house. What does it mean when he finally lets Teddy in? **CHARACTER'S MOTIVATIONS**

*When Dad lets Teddy in, it means* _____

_____

burst

comforted

huddled

journey

opportunities

recognized

# Vocabulary

## Build Robust Vocabulary

Write the Vocabulary Word that completes each sentence in the letters. The first one has been done for you.

Dear Carmen,

Today we left California for our long

**(1)** _____ journey _____ to Ohio.

My little sister feels really bad. Poor Marta

**(2)** _____ into tears when

we drove away. I told her that Dad will have new

job **(3)** _____ in Ohio.

I think knowing that Dad could get a better job

**(4)** _____ Marta. But I still

feel sad for her.

More later,

Eva

Dear Carmen,

After 400 miles, we got a big surprise. Snow! Marta and I **(5)** _____ close to keep warm. Brrrrr! I'm glad you knit me that thick scarf!

Now we are almost to Cleveland. I was born there, but I don't remember it. Mom has already **(6)** _____ some sights along the way and told us about them. Ohio is my new home, so I will try to like it. Write to me soon!

Your best pal,
Eva

# Dear Diary

by Guadalupe V. Lopez • illustrated by Vincent Nguyen

December 14

Dear Diary,

Here I go into the unknown! Today is the start of our journey. I don't want to leave California, but I feel better than poor Marta. My little sister burst into tears and started sobbing as we finished our packing and loaded the car. **1**

## Stop and Think

**1** Why does the diary writer say she is going into the unknown?

*The writer says she is going into the unknown because* _____

_____

_____

Marta was determined to dislike our new home. "Cleveland is cold, Eva," she had declared. "It snows there. I'll miss sunny California." She eased against me, leaning against my knees.

"Marta," I said, in a big sister tone, "this is a hard choice for Papa, too. He has new job opportunities in Cleveland. We'll have new opportunities, too."

I know my words comforted her. I had to be strong for Marta. I realized that I was afraid, too. Mama said it's okay to be a little afraid of the unknown. ❷

## Stop and Think

❷ If *dis-* means "not," what does *dislike* mean?

"Dislike" means _____

_____

_____

December 15

Dear Diary,

Our journey will take more than three days! It's about 2,800 miles. Do you know what happened after only 400 miles? Snow! It was drifting and swirling all around.

A flashing sign alerted us that chains were required, so Papa pulled over. Then Marta woke up. It was funny how her eyes widened as she peered out at the snow.

"What's wrong? What is that?" she asked.

"Snow," Mama replied.

The white flakes were a big surprise for Marta. **3**

## Stop and Think

**3** Why does the snow surprise Marta?

*The snow surprises Marta because* _____

_____

_____

We got out of the car to take a closer look. Snow is cold. I'm glad my friend Carmen knit me this scarf! I wrapped it around my neck snugly. Marta and I huddled together and kept warm as we watched Papa put chains on the tires. They help the tires grip the road and keep the car from slipping.

I was born in Cleveland, but I don't remember snow at all. Mama recognized it right away. She remembered a big snowfall from her childhood. ❹

**Stop and Think**

❹ Why does Papa put chains on the tires?

Papa puts chains on the tires so _____

_____

_____

Mama told us the story. "I was only five years old. My father couldn't find his car because it was mostly under snow! Snowdrifts were six feet high. Dad couldn't get to work, and we couldn't get to school. It was one of the biggest snowstorms ever."

"What did you do with so much snow?" I asked.

"It's fun to play in," smiled Mama.

Papa wrinkled his nose. "It's not fun for grown-ups."

"I know. I know," Mama said and patted his arm. **5**

## Stop and Think

**5** Why do children feel differently about snow than grown-ups do?

*Children feel differently about snow because* _____

_____

_____

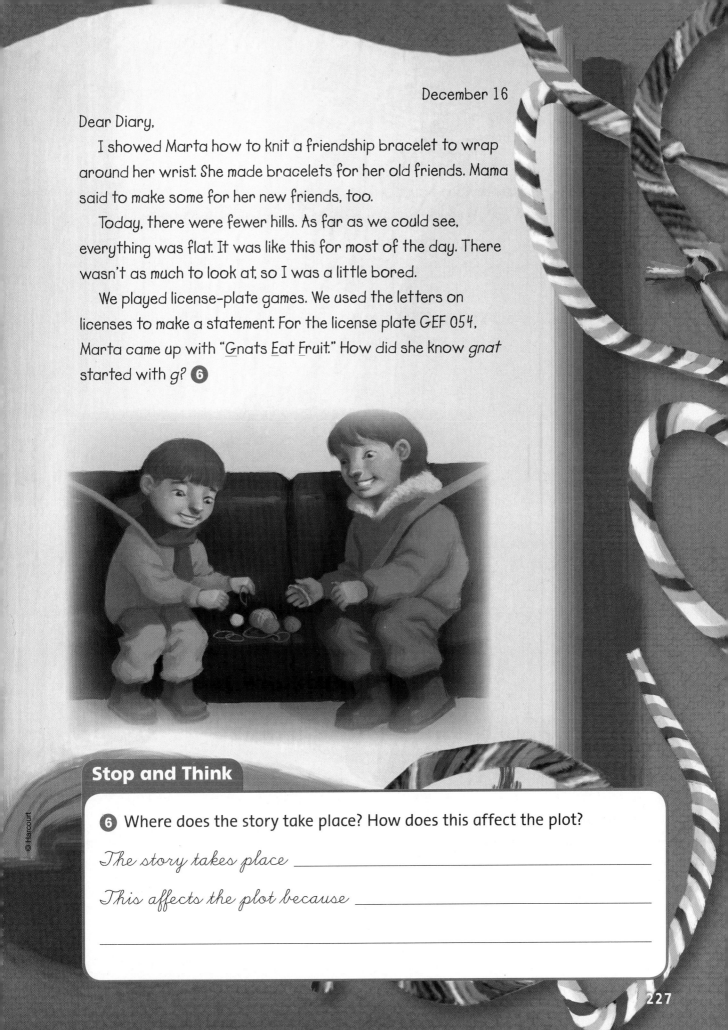

December 16

Dear Diary,

I showed Marta how to knit a friendship bracelet to wrap around her wrist. She made bracelets for her old friends. Mama said to make some for her new friends, too.

Today, there were fewer hills. As far as we could see, everything was flat. It was like this for most of the day. There wasn't as much to look at, so I was a little bored.

We played license-plate games. We used the letters on licenses to make a statement. For the license plate GEF 054, Marta came up with "Gnats Eat Fruit." How did she know *gnat* started with *g*? **6**

## Stop and Think

**6** Where does the story take place? How does this affect the plot?

The story takes place _____

This affects the plot because _____

_____

© Harcourt

Dear Diary,

We are in Cleveland! We got here last night. Papa didn't even knock before Uncle Tony rushed out and hugged us. We hurried into his warm house.

A little girl was there. Her name was Isabel. She strolled right up to Marta. "What took you so long?" she asked. "I've been waiting."

Marta laughed out loud. She took out one of the bracelets she'd made and tied it around Isabel's plump wrist. Isabel liked it.

So far, so good. I'll write more later. **7**

## Stop and Think

**7** Eva and Marta did not want to move to Cleveland. How do you think they feel now? Why?

Now Eva and Marta feel _____

_____

# Think Critically

1. How does the story end? Copy the chart, and fill it in. **CHARACTER, SETTING, PLOT**

```
┌─────────────────┐   ┌─────────────────┐
│   Characters    │   │     Setting     │
└────────┬────────┘   └────────┬────────┘
         │                     │
┌────────┴─────────────────────┴──────────┐
│              Plot Events                 │
│  1. They load the car and leave California. │
│  2. They drive through a snowstorm.      │
│  3. Mama tells about a snowstorm long ago. │
│  4.                                      │
│  5.                                      │
└──────────────────────────────────────────┘
```

2. How does Isabel make Marta laugh? **CHARACTER'S EMOTIONS**

Isabel made Marta laugh when she _____

_____

_____

_____

3. In the beginning, Marta was sad. How does she feel in the end? How do you know? **MAKE COMPARISONS**

In the end, Marta feels _____

_____

_____

_____

fidget

forlornly

noble

pathetic

resolved

scrounging

stingy

suspicion

## Build Robust Vocabulary

Read the story and think about the meanings of the words in dark type.

Phil Cricket bounded from the bus into the city. When he saw a cat in front of him, he froze in his tracks. Phil looked back **forlornly** at the bus. He began to **fidget** as he looked for a way to escape.

As the cat came closer, Phil gave a **pathetic** little squeak. He told the cat he was in the city to find his nephew. He was **resolved** to find him. The cat said his name was Ralph. Phil watched Ralph with **suspicion.**

Ralph offered Phil some crackers. "I found these while I was **scrounging** around," he said. He wasn't **stingy** with food. Ralph said that he would help Phil find his nephew. Phil found the cat to be **noble** and kind.

**Write the Vocabulary Word that completes each sentence. The first one has been done for you.**

1. When the cat came closer, Phil gave a
   _____**pathetic**_____ squeak.

2. Phil looked at the cat with _____ . He didn't trust him yet.

3. Ralph found food by _____ around.

4. Phil began to _____ as he looked for a way to escape.

5. Ralph shared food and said he would help Phil. This made Phil think the cat was _____ and kind.

6. Ralph was not _____ with his food.

7. Phil looked _____ back at the bus when he first saw the cat.

8. Phil was _____ to find his nephew. He would not give up until his nephew was found.

# PHIL IN THE CITY

by Guadalupe V. Lopez • illustrated by Amy Ning

Phil Cricket bounded from the bus and looked around. He saw lots of concrete and lots of feet. At last, this was the city. There was so much to see! He saw a pamphlet on a stand declaring "Places to Visit." This was a start.

All of a sudden, Phil froze in his tracks. A big cat was right in his path. Where did he come from? Do cats eat crickets? Phil gulped and tried to think fast.

Phil looked back forlornly at the bus. No escape there. It was too far away. He began to fidget as he glanced this way and that. ❶

## Stop and Think

❶ Do you think the cat will eat Phil?

*I think the cat will* _____

_____

_____

The cat came closer. Phil gave a pathetic little squeak. "Hello!" exclaimed the cat. "Have you come here for a visit, or perhaps you are here to explore?"

Phil opened one eye. This cat seemed rather sophisticated. "I'm here to find my nephew. He said he needs me. I am resolved to find him."

"Perhaps I can be of some help. Let me introduce myself. I am Ralph."

"My name is Phil," the cricket replied.

"I can help you," Ralph said. "But wait. Where are my manners? Can I get you something to eat?" **2**

## Stop and Think

**2** Think about the sentence "This cat seemed rather sophisticated." Is it a fact or an opinion? Explain your answer.

*This sentence is* _____

_____

_____

Phil watched the cat with suspicion. Cats were supposed to be sneaky, but this one was polite. And he wasn't stingy with his food. Could it be a trick?

"Oh, phooey! I know what you're thinking," mumbled Ralph. "But I'm not being phony. Cats can be mean. But we are not *all* that way."

Phil felt ashamed of himself. "Thank you, Ralph," he replied, "I am starving after my long trip." ❸

## Stop and Think

❸ Why does Ralph say he knows what Phil is thinking?

Ralph says he knows what Phil is thinking because _____

_____

_____

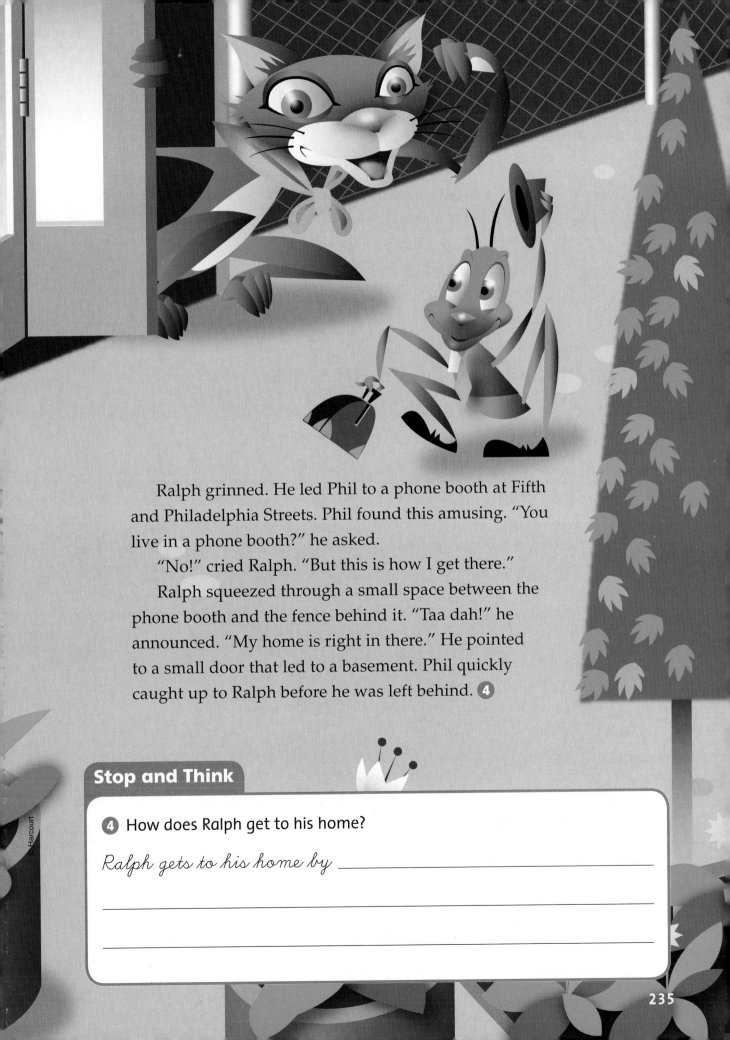

Ralph grinned. He led Phil to a phone booth at Fifth and Philadelphia Streets. Phil found this amusing. "You live in a phone booth?" he asked.

"No!" cried Ralph. "But this is how I get there."

Ralph squeezed through a small space between the phone booth and the fence behind it. "Taa dah!" he announced. "My home is right in there." He pointed to a small door that led to a basement. Phil quickly caught up to Ralph before he was left behind. **4**

## Stop and Think

**4** How does Ralph get to his home?

*Ralph gets to his home by* _____

_____

_____

"This is my home!" exclaimed Ralph with pride. "They sell paper here—newsprint, notebook paper, graph paper. The problem is, mice like paper, too. They shred it to make nests. So that's why I live here. To chase away the mice."

Phil looked around. The space was filled with paper in stacks, on rolls, and in boxes.

Suddenly, Ralph stopped and scurried behind a mound of paper. Phil expected a mouse to pop out at any moment, with Ralph close behind. **5**

## Stop and Think

**5** What happens after Phil discovers he is in a paper warehouse?

*After Phil discovers he is in a paper warehouse,* _____

_____

_____

236

"Aha!" cried Ralph. "Crackers! I found these when I was scrounging around. It's amazing the things one can find if one looks hard enough. Have a bite."

Phil took a cracker. The tasty bit was crispy. Ralph flashed Phil a triumphant smile.

"So, where is your nephew?" asked Ralph.

"Well," replied Phil, "this may sound odd, but he told me to look for an elephant in Phelps Park."

"That's not odd at all!" exclaimed Ralph. "I can take you there." **6**

## Stop and Think

**6** Do you think Phil will find his nephew? Explain your answer.

I think Phil _____

_____

_____

Phil and Ralph rushed off. All of a sudden, Ralph burst into song. Phil started to hum along. He realized that he found Ralph simply amazing.

"Here you are!" declared Ralph. "An elephant in Phelps Park!" Phil looked up. There was his nephew perched on the plastic elephant's back, waving to them.

Phil turned to Ralph and shook his paw. "Thank you," he said. "I've decided cats are noble and kind." Then Phil recalled Ralph's song. "Let me rephrase that. Cats are noble, kind, *and* talented!" **7**

## Stop and Think

**7** In the beginning, Phil felt one way about cats. How does he feel now?

*Phil feels* _____

_____

_____

# Think Critically

**1.** **What happens in the story? Copy the chart, and fill it in.** SEQUENCE

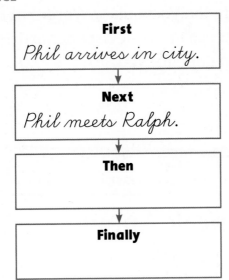

| First |
|---|
| *Phil arrives in city.* |

↓

| Next |
|---|
| *Phil meets Ralph.* |

↓

| Then |
|---|
| |

↓

| Finally |
|---|
| |

**2.** **How do you know that the author wrote this story to entertain you?** AUTHOR'S PURPOSE

*I know the author wrote this story to entertain me*

*because* _____

_____

_____

**3.** **What will Phil tell his nephew about his first day in the city?** PLOT

*Phil will say that* _____

_____

_____

© Harcourt

# Vocabulary

## Build Robust Vocabulary

Write the Vocabulary Word that completes each sentence in the newspaper articles. The first one has been done for you.

---

DAILY NEWS                    SECTION C

## Ranger to Speak About Mangrove Forests

by Bill Wilson                                      Thursday, November 12

---

Ranger Terry Lee will speak tonight at the park shelter. Her focus will be on saving mangrove forests. "The mangrove forest is a truly

**(1)** _____remarkable_____ place,"  said Ranger Lee. "All of us must help protect it."

Ranger Lee said that the mangroves need to be saved from the threats ahead. She warned: "The trees protect us from bad weather and provide food. Mangroves are strong and can **(2)** _____ nasty storms; their biggest enemy is us."

# Kids Learn About Mangroves from Ranger Lee

by Bill Wilson                                                Friday, November 13

Ranger Terry Lee gave a speech about mangrove trees last night. Many children were there.

Ranger Lee described how mangrove trees spread: "Each seed takes

(3) _____ of the

mother tree by staying connected until it gets bigger. As it grows, the seed (4) _____ food from the mother tree. When the new tree is ready, it will drop into the water and be carried away to a new place to grow on its own."

Ranger Lee also taught the kids that mangroves make

(5) _____ homes for many animals.

"Birds nest there," she said, "and birds' eggs are a tasty food for snakes. The (6) _____ rat snake will silently crawl up the mangrove tree to grab eggs from a nest."

Many children agreed that the mangroves need to be protected. One child said, "Now I know how mangrove trees can be saved. I'm glad Ranger Lee taught us about them."

# Where Land and Sea Meet

**by Guadalupe V. Lopez**

Where the land meets the sea, mangrove trees grow. They are some of the world's most unusual trees. They have strong roots like other trees. But their roots don't spread under the ground. Instead, they grow in salt water.

The red mangrove is found along the coast in seawater. This tree has roots that can get fresh water from salt water. The red roots look like long legs. Some think this tree looks as if it's standing or walking in the water! That's why this mangrove is also called the "walking tree." **1**

## Stop and Think

**1** What would you like to learn about mangrove trees?

*I would like to learn* _____

_____

_____

Mangroves have a remarkable way of making new trees. Each tree makes plenty of seeds, about three hundred a year. But these seeds do not fall from the tree. Instead, each seed takes advantage of the mother tree by staying connected. The seed extracts food from the mother tree as it grows.

Over time, the seed grows into a tiny tree. This new tree gets stronger. When it's ready, it will drop into the water below. It may drift away to a new place. When it reaches suitable soil, it will spread its roots and grow. ❷

## Stop and Think

❷ How do mangroves make new trees?

*To make new trees, first mangroves* _____

_____

_____

A mangrove forest is home to many kinds of wildlife. It is the beginning of a food chain for other living things. As the tree grows, its leaves fall. These dead leaves are good food for other animals. Little crabs, fish, and insects eat the leaves. Then small fish and birds eat these animals. Bigger fish, birds, and snakes eat the small ones. Even people catch some of these animals for food! ❸

## Stop and Think

❸ What are some animals that live in a mangrove forest?

*Some animals that live in a mangrove forest are*

_____

_____

244

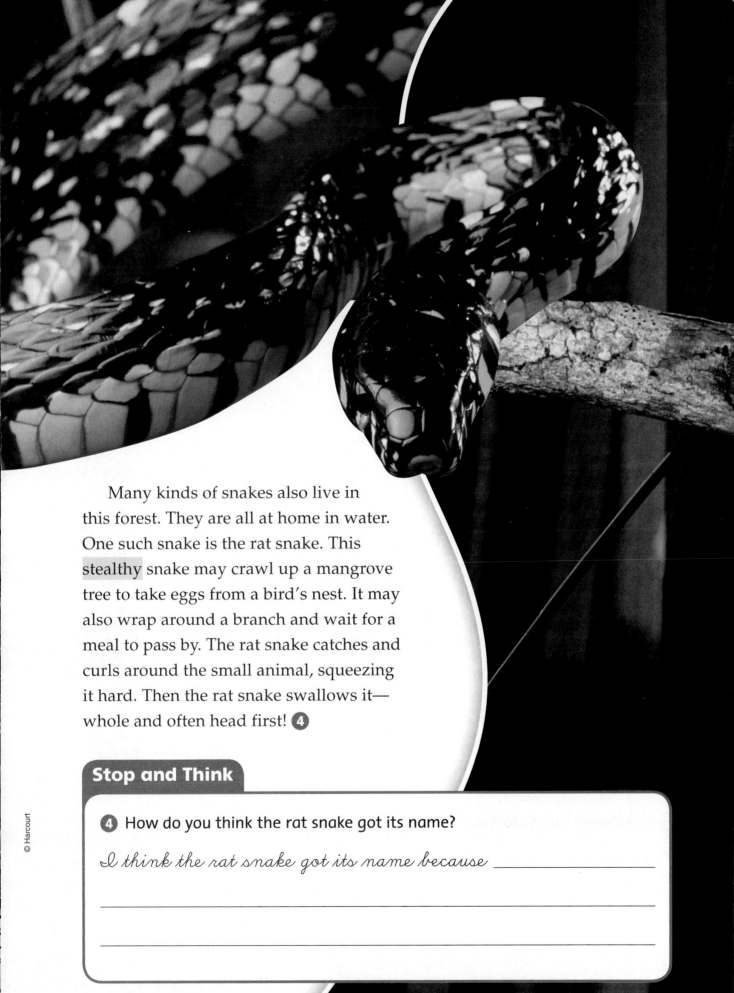

Many kinds of snakes also live in this forest. They are all at home in water. One such snake is the rat snake. This stealthy snake may crawl up a mangrove tree to take eggs from a bird's nest. It may also wrap around a branch and wait for a meal to pass by. The rat snake catches and curls around the small animal, squeezing it hard. Then the rat snake swallows it— whole and often head first! ❹

## Stop and Think

❹ How do you think the rat snake got its name?

*I think the rat snake got its name because* _____

_____

_____

Mangroves are not just animal homes. They also help the land and people who live nearby. The trees stop the land from being slowly washed into the sea. Strong roots keep the soil in place. The roots and tree trunks also protect homes during storms. They block some of the force of the heavy winds. The winds are less strong by the time they reach the homes nearby.

Mangroves can protect against deadly tidal waves. These are huge waves that rush onto the land. The trees help to block the force of the waves. **5**

## Stop and Think

**5** How do mangroves help the land?

*Mangroves help the land by* _____

_____

_____

Mangroves are strong, but they can't withstand all threats. The trees are often cut down so the land can be used for other things. Two of the greatest threats to mangroves are new homes and roads. Many mangrove forests have already begun to disappear. If they *do* disappear, so will the fish, birds, alligators, snakes, shrimp, and other animals that live there. **6**

## Stop and Think

**6** What will happen if mangrove forests disappear?

*If mangrove forests disappear,* _____

_____

_____

247

Many people want to save the mangroves from the threats ahead. They understand that the trees provide food, protect them from threatening weather, and keep the land from washing away. They are taking steps to save the trees.

In some places, people work together to keep these helpful and unusual forests healthy. They understand how important these trees are. They plant new trees so the mangrove forests won't disappear. **7**

## Stop and Think

**7** Is it better to protect the mangroves, or is it better to use the land for homes? Why?

*I think it is better to* _____

_____

_____

# Think Critically

**1.** What have you learned about mangroves? Copy the chart, and fill it in. MAIN IDEA AND DETAILS

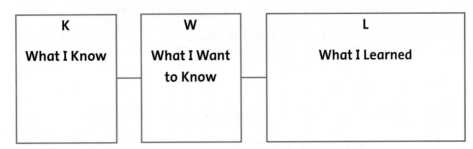

| K | W | L |
|---|---|---|
| **What I Know** | **What I Want to Know** | **What I Learned** |

**2.** What fact about mangroves do you think is the most interesting? EXPRESS PERSONAL OPINIONS

*I think the most interesting fact about mangroves*

*is* _____

_____

_____

**3.** What do you think the author wanted you to learn from this article? AUTHOR'S PURPOSE

*I think the author wanted me to learn that*

_____

_____

_____

# Vocabulary

## Build Robust Vocabulary

Write the word that best completes each sentence.
The first one has been done for you.

**1.** "Hello, travel fans! Today's _____destination_____ is

**misfortune   destination   aspect**

the exciting Monterey County Fair," the

reporter announces.

**2.** Carlos Garza says, "A large crowd is waiting

_____ for the pig races."

**forlornly   vigorously   expectantly**

**3.** Some people think pigs are ugly. They can't

understand why pig racers think their pets are

_____ .

**prideful   gorgeous   ornate**

**4.** One boy is _____

**vigorously   stealthily   forlornly**

scrubbing his pig. He enjoys this job!

**5.** "I'm Ellen Wright at the Arts and Crafts Arena,"

says a second reporter. "Let's look at some

_____ quilts with lots of patterns."

**ornate   pathetic   stingy**

**6.** "The blocks of this quilt have pictures. Each block

_____ something for the people

**huddles   withstands   symbolizes**

who made it," the quilter explains.

**7.** Some of the blocks _____ the

**reconstruct   fidget   intend**

history of a town or neighborhood.

**8.** Besides animals and crafts, an important

_____ of the fair is food!

**suspicion   journey   aspect**

**9.** Carlos says, "Come to this fair if you want to

see a truly _____ sight."

**festive   pathetic   prideful**

**10.** "It will be a great _____

**journey   misfortune   suspicion**

if you miss the fair this year," warns Carlos.

**Write the answers to these questions. Use complete sentences.**

**11.** What does it mean to wait expectantly?

_____

_____

**12.** What aspect of the fair would you like best?

_____

_____

# Monterey County Fair

by Guadalupe V. Lopez
illustrated by Remy Simard

### Cast of Characters

| | |
|---|---|
| Ben Belmont | Carol Cline |
| Carlos Garza | Scott Livingston |
| Ellen Wright | Florence Williams |
| Max | Chuck Wright |

**Ben:** Hello, everyone! I'm Ben Belmont. Welcome to "Explore California." With me is my co-host, Carol Cline.

**Carol:** Today's destination is the city of Monterey. We're at the Monterey County Fair, which offers great entertainment for the entire family.

**Ben:** Let's go to our reporter Carlos Garza at the Livestock Arena. ❶

## Stop and Think

❶ Where are the reporters today?

*Today, the reporters are* _____

_____

_____

© Harcourt

**Carlos:** Hello, Ben and Carol! A large crowd is waiting expectantly for the pig races. I'm here with Scott Livingston, the owner of Reina the Pig. Scott is vigorously scrubbing his gorgeous Reina, and she seems to be enjoying it.

**Scott:** Yes, Reina likes all this fuss over her, but she doesn't like to run. I think she'd rather be pampered, like a queen. In last year's race, she came in eighth.

**Carlos:** No kidding? How many pigs were racing?

**Scott:** Umm, actually, there were eight. ❷

## Stop and Think

❷ In the sentence "In last year's race, she came in eighth," is *race* used as a noun or a verb?

*In this sentence, "race" is* _____

_____

© Harcourt

**Carlos:** That is a misfortune. But you did name her well. Doesn't Reina mean "queen" in Spanish? Maybe Reina will be the "reigning" pig in this year's big event. We'll be here at three o'clock to see Reina race.

**Carol:** Yes, best of luck to them. Now let's visit the Arts and Crafts Arena. Hello, Ellen Wright.

**Ellen:** Hello! All around I see beautiful works of art. Look at this ornate quilt, which took "Best of Show." I'm speaking to Florence Williams, the quiltmaker. Florence, tell us about your quilt. ❸

## Stop and Think

❸ After Carlos does his interview, which reporter is next? Who does he or she interview?

*After Carlos does his interview,* _____

_____

_____

**Florence:** It is an album quilt. An album quilt is made by a group of quilters, in our case, eight quilters. Each block symbolizes something. Sometimes, you can study the blocks and reconstruct the history of a town or neighborhood.

**Ellen:** The eight of you did a great job. Your quilt really is the best in the show. Thanks for sharing it with us. Carol and Ben, back to you. ④

## Stop and Think

④ What is an album quilt? Underline the words that tell you.

*An album quilt is* _____

_____

_____

Ben: Thank you, Ellen. Those quilts sure look festive. Now let's look at another important aspect of Monterey County, agriculture.

Carol: Our reporter Max is at the Food Arena.

Max: Hello, Ben and Carol! Wait until you see this! I'm here with Chuck Wright. He and his neighbors are making a huge salad.

Chuck: We are trying to break a world record, Max. **5**

## Stop and Think

**5** Do you think Chuck and his neighbors will break the world record? Explain your answer.

*I think Chuck and his neighbors* _____

_____

_____

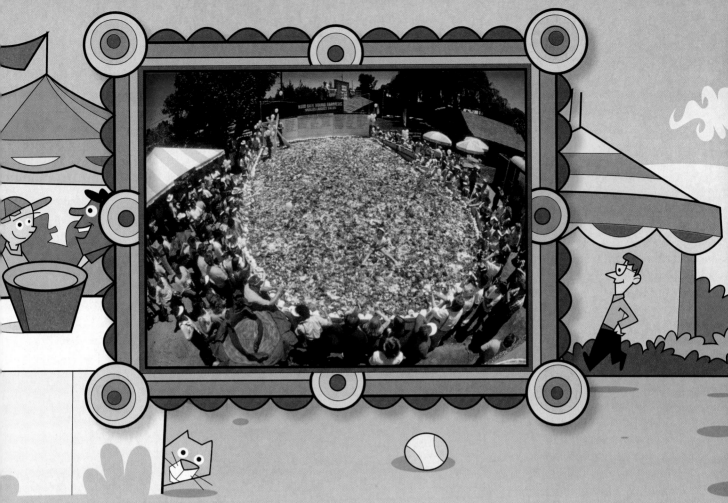

**Max:** What does something like this weigh?

**Chuck:** It weighs more than 29,000 pounds.

**Max:** Wow! May I have some?

**Chuck:** At three o'clock, we'll start serving.

**Max:** I'll come back. Until then, do you know where I can get a nice steak sandwich? I'm starving.

**Chuck:** Yes, there is a great grill right across the way.

**Max:** Ben and Carol, I'm going to grab some lunch. Let's meet at three o'clock for some salad. **6**

## Stop and Think

**6** Name one fact you know about the salad. Then give an opinion you have about salad.

*One fact about the salad is that* _____

_____

_____

**Ben:** Three o'clock? Isn't that the time of the pig race? Bad break, Max. You'll have to choose.

**Carol:** Our time is about up. Come to the fair. You'll have a great time, no matter what you choose to see. The fair runs until Sunday the eighth, so take a break and come see it all.

**Ben:** Thank you for joining us. We'll see you on the next episode of "Explore California"! Until then, enjoy exploring the wonderful Golden State. **7**

## Stop and Think

**7** Find the sentence "Bad break, Max." What does this sentence mean?

*The sentence means* _____

_____

_____

# Think Critically

**1.** The reporter tells people when the fair ends. Why do you think he does this? **MAKE INFERENCES**

*I think the reporter tells people when the fair ends because* _____

_____

_____

**2.** What do you think is the main idea of this play? Why? **MAIN IDEA AND DETAILS**

*I think the main idea of this play is* _____

_____

_____

**3.** How do you think the author feels about going to a county fair? **AUTHOR'S PURPOSE**

*I think the author* _____

_____

_____

© Harcourt

259

complicated

contraptions

eerie

elegant

massive

obstacles

roamed

submerged

# Vocabulary

## Build Robust Vocabulary

Write the Vocabulary Word that completes each sentence. The first one has been done for you.

Have you ever seen a mammoth? You might have seen one in a history book or movie. Mammoths **(1)** _____roamed_____ the earth a long time ago during the Ice Age. Their **(2)** _____ size made them rough and tough beasts.

Mammoths ate plants. Their trunks reached the leaves in trees and pulled plants from the ground. These trunks must have been pleasing to see. They were long and **(3)** _____. Their trunks were also strong enough to knock **(4)** _____ out of the way.

Early humans hunted the mammoth for food. They did not have modern **(5)** _____ like traps and cages to catch them. It must have been a **(6)** _____ task to hunt a mammoth with stone weapons, but that's what they did.

Though no one has seen a living mammoth, we know what they looked like. In 1974, some workers came across giant mammoth bones. What they saw was so **(7)** _____ it sent chills down their spines. The giant bones had been **(8)** _____ in water and layers of mud for thousands of years.

**Write the Vocabulary Word that best completes the synonym web.**

**9.**

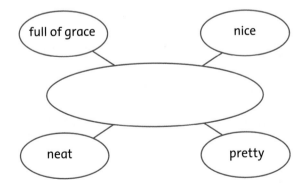

full of grace

nice

neat

pretty

# ROUGH AND TOUGH ENOUGH

by Keith Maynard • illustrated by Laura Jacobsen

Our world is full of rough and tough animals. However, no beast on land these days matches the massive size of a mammoth. Mammoths were rough and tough animals from the past.

Many mammoths roamed Earth during the Ice Age. At that time, most of the land on Earth was frozen. Massive sheets of ice hid most of the ground. Mammoths had to be tough to stand the cold. They had great coats of hair. They also had enough body fat to keep them warm. Each one weighed about 6,000 pounds. **1**

## Stop and Think

**1** Mammoths were large, tough animals from the past. What details support this?

*These details support the main idea:* _____

_____

_____

Though mammoths were rough and tough, they did not hunt. They were plant-eaters. They used their elegant trunks to reach leaves in trees. They were even strong enough to pull plants from the ground. Then they brought the food to their mouths where large, flat teeth ground through the plants.

The trunk had other uses, too. It gave an animal a great sense of smell. It was strong enough to knock obstacles out of the way. Scientists think animals may have locked trunks to say hello. **2**

## Stop and Think

**2** How did mammoths use their trunks?

*Mammoths used their trunks* _____

_____

_____

Mammoths lived together in packs. More than one family made up each pack. Each pack had a leader. The leader was the oldest or strongest mother mammoth in the pack.

Though they roamed in packs, these animals did not always get along. Sometimes they fought with their mighty tusks. The tusks were about 10 feet long and made tough weapons. They were sharp enough to dig through snow and find plants. They were strong enough to lift rocks out of the way. ③

## Stop and Think

**③ Why do you think mammoths roamed in packs?**

I think mammoths roamed in packs because _____

_____

_____

Early humans hunted mammoths throughout the Ice Age. The hunters did not have contraptions, such as fancy traps or cages. Instead, they fought the giant beasts with stone weapons. They ate the meat and used the bones to make weapons and tools.

Many scientists today think that the hunters prized the mammoths. The hunters created paintings in caves that show the mammoths as they really looked. The artists must have known the animals well. **4**

## Stop and Think

**4** Why do you think there are no mammoths today?

*There are no mammoths today because* _____

_____

_____

Though no one has seen a living mammoth, we know how big they were. In 1974, a large number of bones were found in a hill in Hot Springs, South Dakota. At first, workers wanted to put houses on this land. They brought in big trucks to clear the hill. They soon came across something so eerie it sent chills down their spines. They found many giant bones! No one could explain where the bones had come from or to what animal they belonged.

Though the land was now a hill, it had been a deep hole long ago. The hole had filled with spring water and sticky clay. Maybe the animals visited the hole for a drink and got stuck. Though they fought to get out, maybe they could not.

Over time, the spring ran dry. The animal remains were submerged in layers of water and mud. Their bones were not found for thousands of years. Now Hot Springs is one of the best places to learn about the mammoths. **5**

## Stop and Think

**5** Why were the mammoth bones not found for thousands of years?

*They were not found for thousands of years because* _____

_____

_____

The last of these rough and tough animals died long ago. How and why did this happen? We try to make sense of this complicated riddle.

Many scientists think that it got too warm too fast. Plant life began to change or die. Then the mammoths didn't have enough to eat. Perhaps hunters wiped out the animals. We may never know.

Though these animals no longer walk on Earth, they are still a part of our world. We study them to know about the past. Their story can help us protect the rough and tough animals we have today. **6**

**Stop and Think**

**6** Why doesn't the author tell us why mammoths no longer walk on Earth?

The author doesn't tell us why mammoths no longer walk on Earth because _____

_____

# Think Critically

1. What are some details that support the main idea? Copy the chart, and fill it in. **MAIN IDEA AND DETAILS**

| Detail | Detail | Detail |
|---|---|---|

**Main Idea**

*Mammoths were mighty animals from the past.*

2. Why is Hot Springs, South Dakota, a good place to learn about mammoths? **DRAW CONCLUSIONS**

*Hot Springs, South Dakota, is a good place to learn about mammoths because* _____

_____

_____

3. Why did the author write this article? **AUTHOR'S PURPOSE**

*I think the author wrote this article to* _____

_____

# Vocabulary

ancient

cascading

distant

embedded

eroding

glistens

sentries

weary

## Build Robust Vocabulary

Write the Vocabulary Word that completes each sentence in the postcards. The first one has been done for you.

Dear Shawn,

I'm watching the sun rise over this peaceful lake. The water **(1)** _____glistens_____ in the morning light. A river flows out of this lake at one end. I can imagine it **(2)** _____ along its path and over the cliff ahead. It takes a long time for the river to reach the **(3)** _____ sea. It's so still here. I wish you could be here, too.

Your friend,
Marc

Shawn Mills

72 Southridge Drive

Columbus, Ohio 43220

Dear Jonas,

We are going south on the river now. Guess what I can see from our boat? I see two boys fishing. They are so still they look like **(4)** _____ watching over the river. I think that sitting there for such a long time would make me feel very **(5)** _____ . I guess they are used to a slower pace!

Your friend,
Marc

Jonas Hart
1686 Main Street
Columbus, Ohio  43220

Dear Hannah,

Yesterday we saw a huge alligator! It looked as old and **(6)** _____ as the river. It was lying on a big rock **(7)** _____ in the mud. In places, the land on the riverbanks is **(8)** _____ and falling into the water. It makes the water very muddy.

Your friend,
Marc

Hannah Paoletti
2343 Westover Road
Columbus, Ohio  43220

# Along the Mighty Mississippi

## by Shannon Gilliam

The sun rises over a peaceful lake. Water glistens in the morning light. The lake is fairly small, but it has a big job. It is the start of the Mississippi River.

It's not easy to tell exactly where the lake ends or where, exactly, the river begins. Water is restless. It is always flowing, but look carefully. You will see some of it slip away. It flows into a nearby stream.

The mighty river starts out timidly. It makes its way north and east. As the river bends south, it quickly picks up speed. Soon, it is tumbling over cascading rapids along its path to the sea. It will flow through ten states in all. **1**

## Stop and Think

**1** The Mississippi River flows through ten states in all. What are some details that support this main idea?

*Some details that support the main idea are* _____

_____

_____

Minnesota

Lake Itasca

Wisconsin

Iowa

Mississippi River

Missouri River

Illinois

Ohio River

Kentucky

Missouri

Arkansas

Tennessee

Arkansas River

Mississippi River

Mississippi

Louisiana

Gulf of Mexico

© Harcourt

273

High above, birds soar over the water. They can see the distant river clearly. In the late fall, the river serves as a map for birds. They follow it to reach warmer places.

Nearby, two boys settle in a comfortable place to go fishing. Quietly, they dip their lines into the river. They sit like sentries as the endless water flows by.

The river has roughly 250 kinds of fish. Along this part of the river, the boys may catch bass or trout. Different fish are found farther south. **2**

## Stop and Think

**2** Why does the author share facts about the river's fish?

*The author shares facts about the river's fish because* _____

_____

_____

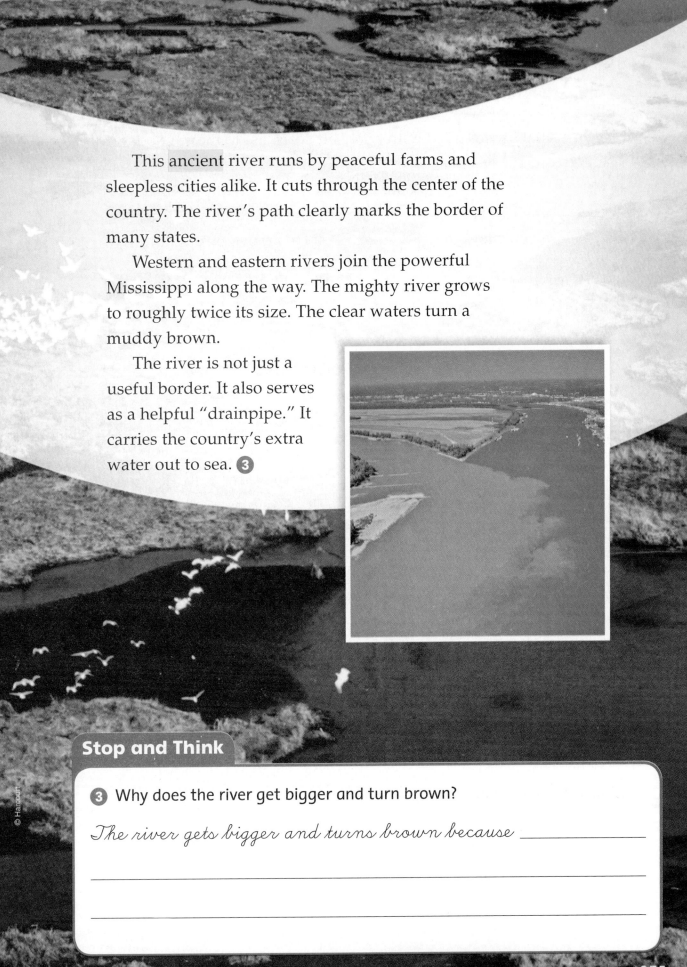

This ancient river runs by peaceful farms and sleepless cities alike. It cuts through the center of the country. The river's path clearly marks the border of many states.

Western and eastern rivers join the powerful Mississippi along the way. The mighty river grows to roughly twice its size. The clear waters turn a muddy brown.

The river is not just a useful border. It also serves as a helpful "drainpipe." It carries the country's extra water out to sea. ❸

## Stop and Think

❸ Why does the river get bigger and turn brown?

*The river gets bigger and turns brown because* _____

_____

_____

The river is also a useful way to move goods. In the past, steamboats moved goods up and down the river. Now, powerful tugboats do the job. They push and pull flat barges filled with goods. It costs less to move goods this way.

Visitors in St. Louis stop to watch. It's afternoon, and the sun beats down on the hot and weary crowd. The water flows quickly here. The boats move through the water, cutting an effortless path across the river. **4**

## Stop and Think

**4** Why is the river a useful way to ship goods?

*The river is a useful way to ship goods because* _____

_____

_____

Near the river's end, the water splits into countless channels. The river flows more slowly here. The land is wet all around. This is the river's last stop on its way to the sea.

An alligator quietly crawls over rocks embedded in the mud nearby. He's careful not to make a sound. He's hopeful for a good catch for dinner.

This part of the country is known as the delta. It changes over time. The land is always eroding as the river flows over it in new ways. **5**

## Stop and Think

**5** Where do you think the article will take us next?

I think the article will take us _____

_____

_____

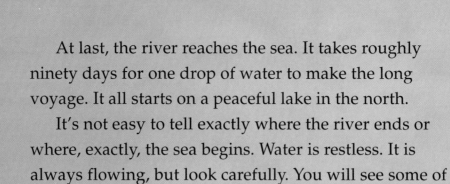

At last, the river reaches the sea. It takes roughly ninety days for one drop of water to make the long voyage. It all starts on a peaceful lake in the north.

It's not easy to tell exactly where the river ends or where, exactly, the sea begins. Water is restless. It is always flowing, but look carefully. You will see some of it slipping away. **6**

**Stop and Think**

**6** How is the end of the article like the beginning?

*The end of the article is like the beginning because* _____

_____

_____

# Think Critically

**1.** What is this article mostly about? Copy the chart, and fill it in.

MAIN IDEA AND DETAILS

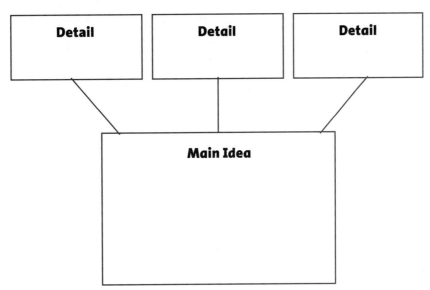

**2.** What happens once a drop of water joins the river?

CAUSE AND EFFECT

*Once a drop of water joins the river, _____*

_____

_____

**3.** Did the author write this story to entertain you or to give you facts? Explain your answer. AUTHOR'S PURPOSE

*The author wrote the story to _____*

_____

_____

behemoth

colossal

cordially

fanciful

hearty

illusion

scenic

# Vocabulary

## Build Robust Vocabulary

Write the Vocabulary Word that completes each sentence. The first one has been done for you.

There have been many **(1)** _____fanciful_____ stories told about the Wild West, but none is as great as the story of Texas Kate. She was born long ago in a **(2)** _____ valley with charming sights to see.

One time, Kate was on her way down south to see her brother, Bill. During the trip, Kate grew to be more than ten feet tall! A girl of Kate's **(3)** _____ size had to eat a lot. She needed a **(4)** _____ meal, so she stopped in a small town along the way.

"What a **(5)** _____ woman!" said

the town's innkeeper when he saw how big Kate was.

Some thought she was an **(6)** _____ ,

but Kate was real. People gave Kate food, but it

disappeared fast and she **(7)** _____

asked for more. The entire town had to help feed Kate.

Kate repaid the town's kindness by helping with

repairs and lifting heavy things. She rebuilt the

town so any size person could live there.

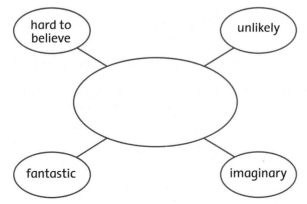

**Write the Vocabulary Word that best completes
the synonym web.**

**8.**

hard to
believe

unlikely

fantastic

imaginary

# The Untold Story of Texas Kate

by Amy Vu • illustrated by Kenneth Vincent

Many a fanciful story has been passed down about the cowboys of the Old West. You may recall a tall tale about Pecos Bill. Pecos Bill was so big he could play with bears and so strong he could ride a mountain lion. But have you ever heard of his little sister, Kate?

Kate's story has been untold for decades. Some say lightning will strike if someone so much as murmurs her name. Nonsense! But gather in quickly as I begin. Looks like some nasty storm clouds are heading this way. ❶

## Stop and Think

❶ What do we know about Kate? Underline the words on the page that tell you.

*Kate is* _____

_____

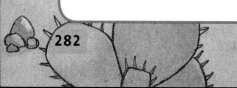

Kate was born in a scenic valley long ago. When she was a teen, her parents thought it was best to head west. But Kate disagreed. Her older brother Bill was down south. She had been most unhappy without Bill around, and so she decided to join him.

Kate started her journey early one day. She loaded her stuff into a big trunk and set off. Before long, she discovered a winding river blocking her path. Then she saw a snake sunning itself nearby, and that gave her an idea. "My voyage is not impossible," declared Kate. She used her trunk, some sticks, her jacket, and a nearby snake to rig up a boat in an instant. **2**

## Stop and Think

**2** Why does Kate head south?

Kate heads south because _____

_____

_____

283

Upon reaching a small town, Kate hopped out. She was not surprised to discover that she'd grown. Time spent on the river, after all, is unlike time on land. She was surprised to see how *much* she'd grown! After being in her boat for so long, Kate had to unfold her arms and legs. She had grown to an impossible size, over ten feet tall!

But Kate didn't want to fret about such things. Instead, food was on her mind. "I need a meal," she exclaimed.

"And a hearty one by the looks of it!" said a no-nonsense fellow sitting nearby. **3**

**Stop and Think**

**3** How does Kate feel when she sees how much she's grown?

When she sees how much she has grown, Kate _____

_____

_____

Kate had not eaten for days. And she was as parched as a fish out of water.

"Come into town," said the man. "We'll get you fed."

Kate could tell this man was not a dishonest fellow. They each introduced themselves, and Kate followed him into town. **4**

## Stop and Think

**4** How does the author describe Kate's thirst? What does this mean?

The author says Kate is _____

_____

_____

The town had everything a girl of Kate's colossal size might need. First, they came across the town's old circus grounds.

"Here is some cloth to replace my clothes," said Kate.

She made the tents into a shirt and pants. She used a tightrope for a belt. Now, she no longer felt improperly dressed. Next, the two friends went to an inn at the center of town.

"What a behemoth woman!" cried the innkeeper. "I have no bed for her."

"Nonsense," cried Kate. "I can sleep out back." **5**

## Stop and Think

**5** What do you think Kate will do next?

*I think Kate will* _____

_____

_____

"Now for my meal," declared Kate.

Her friend gave her a sandwich. Kate popped it
in her mouth, and it was gone in a flash. "I hate to be
impolite," she said cordially. "But I'll need much more
to eat than that."

Her clever friend asked the entire town to help. It
took three days to take care of Kate's huge hunger.

Kate repaid this kindness by helping around the
town. She repaired things too tall for others to reach. She
lifted objects too heavy for most. Kate rebuilt the town so
that anyone of any size could live there. **6**

## Stop and Think

**6** How does Kate's friend help her?

*Kate's friend helps her when he* _____

_____

_____

Kate lived in that town for many years, but she didn't feel settled. One day, she announced it was time to say good-bye. Her new friends were disappointed. But Kate said they simply had to holler her name, and she'd come running. And with that, Kate rode the next tornado right out of town.

So that's the story of Texas Kate. Some say it's untrue. But I saw it all with my very own eyes. You see, I was that no-nonsense fellow she met by the river. And believe me, Kate was no illusion. In fact, sometimes I still hear loud rumbling when she gets really hungry. Some say it's a clap of thunder, but I know better! **7**

## Stop and Think

**7** What do you find out about the narrator on this page?

*I found out that the narrator is* _____

_____

_____

© Harcourt

288

# Think Critically

**1.** Why does Kate leave at the end of the story? Copy the chart, and fill it in. **CAUSE AND EFFECT**

| Cause | Effect |
|-------|--------|
|  | She rides a tornado out of town. |

**2.** What does Kate tell her new friends when she learns they are disappointed that she is leaving? **PLOT**

*Kate tells her new friends* _____

_____

_____

**3.** How would you describe Kate? **CHARACTER'S TRAITS**

*Kate is* _____

_____

_____

_____

| |
|---|
| coddled |
| dainty |
| dedicated |
| determined |
| endured |
| memorable |
| pitiful |

# Vocabulary

## Build Robust Vocabulary

Write the Vocabulary Word that completes each sentence in the diary. The first one has been done for you.

Saturday

When I agreed to go on this trip to the South Pole, I knew I would not be **(1)** _____coddled_____ or treated specially. In fact, we have **(2)** _____ many hardships. Our ship ran into the ice packs right away, and the situation looks tough. But we will try everything we can to finish this task. We are a very

**(3)** _____ crew,

Monday

Our chances are looking **(4)** _____ now. Our ship is trapped in the ice. Can we escape? Will we live to share our tale? Only time will tell.

Thursday

The ice is pressing in on us. Our ship is not small and **(5)** _____ . But how long can it resist the terrible pressure of the ice? The entire crew is totally **(6)** _____ to our boss. I know he can lead us out of this mess. When we finally arrive home and greet our families again, it will be the most **(7)** _____ day of my life.

# Caught in the Ice!

by Shannon Gilliam

His name was Sir Ernest Henry Shackleton. We called him The Boss. He led our ship's expedition to the South Pole. It was a trip marked with problems from the very start.

The ship set sail from South Georgia Island in the South Atlantic Ocean in 1914. We knew it would be no vacation. It would take hard work. We wouldn't be coddled. Still, it was an opportunity for sailors like us to make money.

The first few days were like one fantastic celebration. Few had traveled to the South Pole. We felt fortunate to be a part of this voyage. We'd make history, but we had no idea what was in store for us. ❶

## Stop and Think

❶ Who is telling this story?

*The story is told by* _____

_____

_____

Our ship came across ice packs right away, but we were **determined** sailors. We picked a path through them, avoiding any collision. It was a month of slow sailing.

We expected some ice, but not this much. Soon, the icy sheets froze all around us.

Our ship was like a fly trapped in a frozen spider's web. We saw ice and only ice for miles in every direction. Our earlier celebrations turned into apprehension and fear. The sailors became tense. **2**

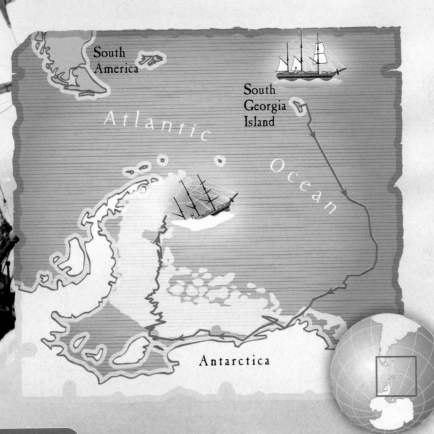

## Stop and Think

**2** Find the simile on this page. What does the author really mean?

This is the simile on this page: _____

It means _____

_____

The Boss put me in charge of keeping everyone happy. I had to keep things light. This was not an easy job, given our ship's pitiful situation.

I would have to use some persuasion to keep everyone happy. I told my fellow sailors we could work together, or we could perish together. That grabbed their attention! Tensions eased, and we began to work as a team.

Still, there were only so many tasks to do on the ship. Each sailor had to keep his station clean. We went on daily hunting expeditions. Most of the time, we just waited for the ice to break up. ③

© Harcourt

## Stop and Think

③ What caused the sailors to work like a team?

*The sailors worked like a team because* _____

_____

_____

294

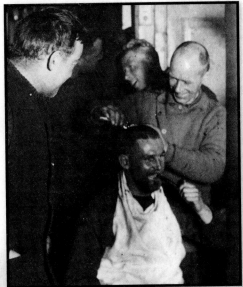

The sailors were men of action. I held more games and contests than I could count. I found a good location for a soccer field on the ice. We played nearly every day. We also had doghouse contests. The men made ice houses for the sled dogs on board. I inspected each shelter and gave prizes for the best one.

Games were the big attraction inside the ship, too. We held haircutting contests. The barbers gave us all funny haircuts until you couldn't look at a man without laughing. At night, the sailors put on plays. They made costumes out of worn shirts and even charged admission. **4**

## Stop and Think

**4** What did the sailors do to keep busy?

*To keep busy, the sailors* _____

_____

_____

One day we had a party. The sailors played music on instruments they'd created by hand. They sounded so dreadful that the sled dogs started howling! It was a **memorable** day, but the celebration did not last. Our luck was running out.

As the months went by, the ice pressed against the ship. Our ship was not at all **dainty**, but it was no match for the pressure of the ice. The ship began to split apart. The noisy creaks and cracking grew louder each day. In the end, we were left with a pile of scrap wood and no ship to sail. **5**

## Stop and Think

**5** What do you think the sailors will do without their ship?

I think the sailors will _____

_____

_____

The ship had been our protection from the cold. Now all we had left were three small boats, five tents, and a collection of tools.

The Boss made a decision. We would march over the ice until we got to open water, dragging our small boats behind us. We were dedicated to our leader, so we followed this decision without question.

The trip was difficult. The boats were small, but heavy. We marched and set up camp in the worst possible conditions. It took months, but we finally made it to the open water. **6**

## Stop and Think

**6** What did the sailors do after they lost their ship?

*After the sailors lost their ship, they* _____

_____

_____

We had endured so much, yet it was not over. We found our way over choppy waters to tiny Elephant Island. It wasn't a great location. We couldn't stay long.

The Boss decided to head out again for help. He selected five men to take with him on this risky mission. The water was rough, and help was far away. We didn't know if we would ever see them again.

Finally, on August 30, 1916, a ship was spotted far out on the horizon. The Boss had returned! We'd been gone for nearly two years. Yet every sailor survived the harsh conditions. Against all odds, The Boss brought us home safe and sound. **7**

## Stop and Think

**7** Why do you think the author wrote about this expedition?

*I think the author wrote about this expedition because* _____
_____
_____

© Harcourt

# Think Critically

**1.** Tell what happens after the sailors land on Elephant Island. Copy the chart, and fill it in. **SEQUENCE/MAIN IDEA AND DETAILS**

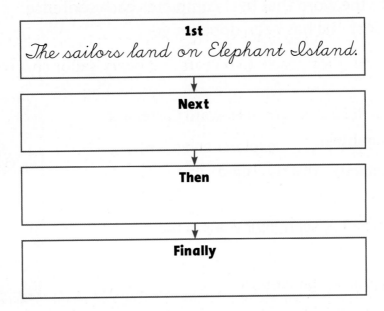

**1st**
The sailors land on Elephant Island.

↓

**Next**

↓

**Then**

↓

**Finally**

**2.** Why did the men march across the ice with the small boats? **CAUSE AND EFFECT**

The men marched across the ice with the small boats

because _____

_____

**3.** How would you describe The Boss? **CHARACTER'S TRAITS**

The Boss is _____

_____

_____

# Vocabulary

## Build Robust Vocabulary

Write the word that best completes each sentence.
The first one has been done for you.

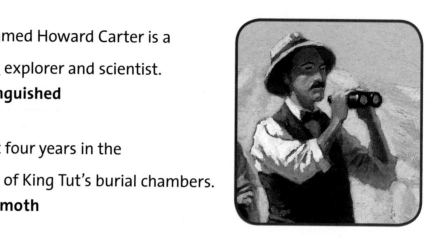

1. It is the year 1922. The famed Howard Carter is a
   _____**distinguished**_____ explorer and scientist.
   **dainty   dubious   distinguished**

2. Howard Carter has spent four years in the
   _____ of King Tut's burial chambers.
   **illusion   vicinity   behemoth**

3. Many scientists doubt his _____
   **dubious   distinguished   weary**
   mission, but Carter pushes on.

4. Carter thinks King Tut's chamber is located beneath the
   sands, but he must _____ this.
   **verify   submerge   cascade**

5. Carter wants his workers to dig in an orderly way, not
   out of control and _____.
   **cordially   abruptly   frantically**

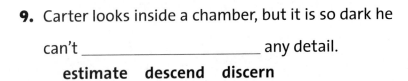

**6.** Carter stops his work _____ when

**cordially   fancifully   abruptly**

the water bearer suddenly runs up to him.

**7.** The boy leads Carter to his digging spot, where Carter

begins to _____ the sand carefully.

**discern   scrutinize   descend**

**8.** After three weeks of hard digging, Carter and his crew

_____ the steps.

**descend   endure   complicate**

**9.** Carter looks inside a chamber, but it is so dark he

can't _____ any detail.

**estimate   descend   discern**

**10.** If Carter finds any objects there, he will have to

_____ their value.

**scrutinize   estimate   descend**

**Write the answers to these questions. Use complete sentences.**

**11.** What does it mean if someone feels that a mission is dubious?

_____

_____

**12.** How would it look if someone was doing something frantically?

_____

_____

# BENEATH THE SANDS

by Shannon Gilliam ≈ illustrated by Scott Cameron

## CHARACTERS

Narrator 1 ≈ Narrator 2 ≈ Narrator 3
Howard Carter, a British excavator in Egypt
Crew Member 1 ≈ Crew Member 2 ≈ Water Bearer
Lord Carnarvon, wealthy British investor
Lady Herbert, the investor's daughter

**Narrator 1:** It is a November afternoon in 1922. Howard Carter is in Egypt, doing what he does best. He is scanning the dunes, digging, recording his finds, and digging some more.

**Narrator 2:** After carefully studying maps of the area, Carter has spent the past four years in this vicinity. He is hoping to locate King Tut's chambers under the sand. ❶

## Stop and Think

❶ What does Carter hope to find in Egypt?

Carter hopes to find _____

_____

_____

**Narrator 3:** Scientists have searched the same drifting sands and have simply given up. They don't believe Carter will ever finish his dubious mission.

**Narrator 1:** We join Carter just before the moment when he will show that they are wrong.

**Carter:** My distinguished career will be over if I don't find King Tut's chambers this year.

**Crew Member 1:** At least we found some huts a few years ago.

**Carter:** Huts are not enough for Lord Carnarvon. He is getting tired of throwing money at our excavation. **2**

## Stop and Think

**2** What does Carter mean by the phrase "throwing money"?

*Carter means* _____

_____

_____

**Crew Member 2:** So this is our last chance?

**Carter:** I'm afraid it is. It's time to be alert.

**Crew Member 1:** Well, we have a fine team of workers. Look, even the youth who brings water is hard at work. Look how fast he is running!

**Carter:** I say! We can't have workers running around frantically. We need to keep an orderly dig.

**Water Bearer:** Mr. Carter! Mr. Carter!

**Carter:** You found something? What is it?

**Water Bearer:** I don't know. I found it when I dug a hole for my water jar. I will show you. ③

## Stop and Think

③ Why does the water bearer run to Carter?

*The water bearer runs to Carter because* _____

_____

_____

**Narrator 2:** Carter stops his work abruptly and follows the lad. Might this new clue lead him to the king?

**Narrator 3:** He begins to scrutinize the sand carefully. Then his eyes widen. He springs into the air and cries out.

**Carter:** This is it! This has to be it!

**Crew Member 2:** Is it the clue we are looking for?

**Carter:** Yes. It is a step carved into the bedrock. The king's chambers must lie below.

**Crew Member 1:** Let's get digging!

**Narrator 1:** At last, they locate a sealed door at the bottom of the steps. Carter sends a note to Lord Carnarvon. **4**

## Stop and Think

**4** What do Carter and his crew do after finding the step?

*After finding the step, Carter and his crew* _____

_____

_____

**Narrator 2:** Now we join the group three weeks later. They have knocked out the first door to find a long hall and a second sealed door. They prepare to open it for the first time.

**Lady Herbert:** What an effort! There are so many steps to descend! It looks like the grand stairs to a ballroom.

**Lord Carnarvon:** But what will we find behind this door? There may be nothing but empty space.

**Lady Herbert:** Or even worse. We could find a third door. **5**

## Stop and Think

**5** What do you think the group will find?

*I think the group will find* _____

_____

_____

© Harcourt

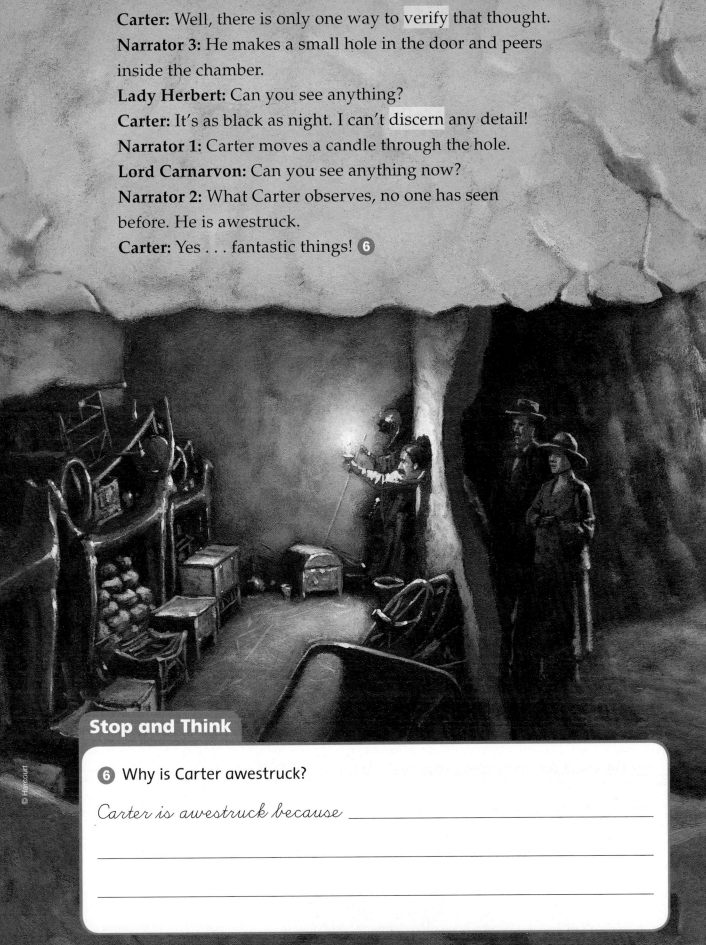

**Carter:** Well, there is only one way to verify that thought.

**Narrator 3:** He makes a small hole in the door and peers inside the chamber.

**Lady Herbert:** Can you see anything?

**Carter:** It's as black as night. I can't discern any detail!

**Narrator 1:** Carter moves a candle through the hole.

**Lord Carnarvon:** Can you see anything now?

**Narrator 2:** What Carter observes, no one has seen before. He is awestruck.

**Carter:** Yes . . . fantastic things! **6**

## Stop and Think

**6** Why is Carter awestruck?

Carter is awestruck because _____

_____

_____

**Narrator 3:** Carter has found something big. But he can't begin to estimate the objects' value.

**Narrator 1:** The four chambers they find behind the door are filled with priceless objects. All are more than three thousand years old. They have to be handled very carefully.

**Narrator 2:** Carter spends the rest of his life writing notes about his great find. His mission is a success. He has found a golden world that for centuries has been hidden beneath the sands! **7**

## Stop and Think

**7** How do you think the author feels about Carter's discovery?

*I think the author feels* _____

_____

_____

# Think Critically

**1.** How would you describe Howard Carter? **CHARACTER**

Howard Carter is _____

_____

_____

**2.** What details does the author give about Carter's discovery?
**MAIN IDEA AND DETAILS**

These are some details the author gives about Carter's

discovery: _____

_____

_____

_____

**3.** What do you think the author wants you to learn from this
story? **AUTHOR'S PURPOSE**

I think the author wants me to learn _____

_____

_____

_____